Victor Koivumäki,
Lake Norden, So'. Dak.

Received
September 16, 1932.

August, 1932, Book.

Address also:
Ely, Minn.

The Road He Trod

The Road He Trod

A Spiritual Pilgrimage

BY

PAUL ZELLER STRODACH

✠

FALCON PRESS
INC.
1451 BROADWAY, NEW YORK

Printed by the Haddon Craftsmen
Camden, N. J., U. S. A.

Contents

[v]

CONTENTS

CONTENTS

The Call

Prepare ye, the way of the Lord
Make straight in the desert a

HIGHWAY

for

our

GOD

✠

The Announcement

Behold
WE
go up to Jerusalem
and all things that are written by the prophets
concerning
THE SON OF MAN
shall be
ACCOMPLISHED

The Invitation

Follow
THOU
ME!

Heart's Desire

WE
would see
JESUS

The Approach

✠

GOD so loved the world, that he gave his only begotten Son, that whosoever believeth in him should not perish, but have everlasting life.

WE see JESUS, who was made a little lower than the angels for the suffering of death, crowned with glory and honor; that he by the grace of GOD should taste death for every man.

CHRIST JESUS, who being in the form of God, thought it not robbery to be equal with God: but made himself of no reputation, and took upon him the form of a servant, and was made in the likeness of men: and being found in fashion as a man, he humbled himself, and became obedient unto death, even the death of the cross.

LOOKING unto JESUS the author and finisher of our faith; who for the joy that was set before him endured the cross, despising the shame, and is set down at the right hand of the throne of GOD.

GOD forbid that I should glory, save in the cross of

our Lord JESUS CHRIST, by whom the world is crucified unto me, and I unto the world.

GOD also hath highly exalted him, and given him a name which is above every name: that at the name of JESUS every knee should bow, of things in heaven, and things in earth, and things under the earth; and that every tongue should confess that JESUS CHRIST is Lord, to the glory of God the Father.

AND when I saw him, I fell at his feet as dead. And he laid his right hand upon me, saying unto me, Fear not; I am the first and the last: I am he that liveth, and was dead; and, behold, I am alive for evermore. Amen.

WHEREFORE he is able to save them to the uttermost who come to GOD by him, seeing he ever liveth to make intercession for them.

The Ultimate

That
I
may know
HIM
and the power of his
RESURRECTION
and the fellowship of his
SUFFERINGS
being made conformable unto
HIS DEATH

Today—and Every Day

✠

I PRAY thee grant me strength to take
   My daily cross, whate'er it be,
And gladly for thine own dear sake
   In paths of life to follow thee.

As on my daily way I go,
   Through light or shade, in calm or strife,
O may I bear thy marks below
   In conquered sin and chastened life.

And week by week this day I ask
   That holy memories of thy Cross
May sanctify each common task,
   And turn to gain each earthly loss.

✠

Thus may I glory in the cross,
   Thy Cross and mine,—but mine for thee;
Full life of praise, and every loss
   Enrichment of thy life in me.

In the Beginning

✛

INSPIRATION : *Read*—GENESIS 1-3

✛

MEDITATION

GOD made Him a world: with all the purpose and goodwill and beauties of the Mind of God did He order and grace and complete it.

Then God made Him a Garden and planted it. Behold, the sunbeams danced from leaf to flower; the waters tinkled and babbled through shade and meadow; the birds sang their happy songs; the creatures of field and woodland browsed and idled 'mid new-born peace and quiet.

Now into this Garden God brought Him Man and Woman that He had created to enjoy and steward all that He had called good. Behold, God had created man in His own Image and had breathed into him His breath, and, behold, he became a living soul endowed with all the gifts of unstinting divine giving, for in the Image of God created He him. And in this Garden and with this Man and this Woman God founded the first Home. And, behold, it was very good: God and Man as one in peace in God's Garden-Home.

Now in the Garden God had planted Him a Tree:

full rich was the beauty and shade thereof, but the glory of the fruit it bore was its crown. Hither brought the Giver Man, and there made He him the Gift of His creative bounty:—All that He had made, save the fruit of that Tree, behold, it was his to have and use. Its beauty might he enjoy; 'neath its shade might he live; but its fruit might he not have. God's Tree;— His Man was to guard it, and enjoy it, but not eat of it. Thus God made Him a Rule of Life for the Garden-Home near the Tree. And Man with the smile of the Image of God on his face knew only to do His will. And there was peace.

But, behold, the Tree of God became the Tree of Desire! and to the voice of the Stranger, Man and Woman listen; and, reaching into its glory, pluck of the fruit and eat. Forbidden desire has been satisfied; and, behold, Man has brought forth disobedience. The Stranger is known: his name is named, and so is the gift *he* has given Man: Satan and Sin. The Man is known: his name is named and so is the gift he has given God: Mortal and Disobedience. God is known: His Name is named and so is the gift He takes from Man: Judge and Life. And now there is no peace.

The Garden is empty of the Home-makers, and lonely is He that walketh therein in the cool of the day. Sorrow and mourning, and sin and death are strangers there, and may not dwell therein. God's sorrow! Man's mourning! Separation, exile, and the road is hard and away from the Garden-Home near the Tree of God and the Tree of Life.

Long years pass. Time stores them away, century on century. Man keeps on, *must* travel on, and take the road away from the Garden-Home. Sorrow and mourning and toil and sin and death are his road-companions. The image of man!—remade by the no longer Stranger. What a "creation"!

Patiently God has filled up His time, too. His heart of sorrow has always been one of love and longing and purpose. Behold, He longs for the coming home of His children of Man, and will make them a Way, and bid them to it.

So God made Him a Hill. It had waited long for Him to do His planting there. Behold, it had no beauty, and men did not desire it; but God chose it! And there planted Him another Tree in the sight of Man, full deep and wide and high and long; and on it God brought forth Fruit, and, behold, the Glory of It outshone the glory of the First Tree. Hither brought the Giver Man, and there made He him the Gift of the Fruit thereof. The Tree to be Desired; of its Fruit to eat and live; 'neath Its shade to lose his burdens; in Its cool to find his powers; under Its protection to build his lasting Home.

And there is Peace!

Resolution

✢

INSPIRATION : *I will go unto the altar of God. . . .*

✢

MEDITATION

THE Tree of Life that God has planted on Golgotha.

Behold, God built Him an Altar . . . Man would not! And God provided Him a Lamb of Sacrifice . . . Man could not!

Mystery sublime! Love transcendant! Gift supreme! Sacrifice and Will Divine!

Why?

God so loved the world . . . behold, the Garden was an empty, lonely place! . . . and the Way is opened by Him to return Home,—the Garden-Home, —the Sepulchre Garden? Yes, that is the Way:—Over the Hill, down through the Garden, HOME!

So I take up my Journey to go to this Altar of God . . . *God my exceeding joy!* And I purpose to travel along the Way with the Traveler, for has He not bid me follow Him?

May He keep me close to Him all the Way . . . all the Way Home.

And how will I make my Journey? First, I will think

[4]

of Him daily, and in meditation seek to fellowship with Him.

Then, quietly I will bring Him what I have, the best I have, all that I have: my devotion, my adoration, my self-consecration. May the little altar that I build him daily be a beauty of holiness, and my sacrifice of love, my prayers and praises, rise a sweet smelling incense unto Him. Amen.

My objective is *His* Altar, these days . . . and every day. And I want to go in holy joy, filled with holy purpose. The best that I have to give Him will not repay His Giving; but joy will be His if I am ever taking more from Him—plucking Fruit from His Tree! For my Best Friend calls me, bids me, urges me, to eat of *this* Tree and live! So I would add daily riches to my heart and soul; by His grace learn and grow, seek and find; amass His wealth in character and service; find my life in living His Life.

The Gate-Way to the Passion

✠

INSPIRATION : *Read*—St. Luke 18:31-43

✠

MEDITATION

A ND Jesus *entered* and *passed through* Jericho."
What eloquent words for this day which be-
gins my pilgrimage—with Jesus. Does He not say to
me, "Behold, *we* go up to Jerusalem?"

Three things are in this little sentence; two are apparent instantly; but the third is hidden away between
the other two. The first is the Gate-way In; the second is the Gate-way Out; but the third is the Cross-
roads! Christ at the Cross-roads!—and I am journeying
along.

That Gate-way In, how inviting: broad, wide open,
beckoning to the lure, the mystery, the adventure, the
life of the city's streets; crowded, teeming with all sorts
and conditions of men: traveler, caravan, priest and
publican, Pharisee and beggar, pilgrim and lolling on-
looker, wayside denizen . . . the gutter man, blind,
unkempt, ragged misery; the noises, the commotion,
the excitement, the babble of sound, the cries,—above
it all, that one that will be heard, "JESUS . . . have
mercy . . . on me."

In the midst of this Broad Highway, of this sunlit

peopled day, the Divine Pilgrim hears; meets the cry; answers the soul; stills the need; heals, harvests, glorifies . . . a man!

Broad, open, inviting, beckoning way, this gate-way today to the World of the Passion: mystery, soul-adventure, Life! Keen to go forward! But before I enter in, here in the broad and so easy-looking way, let me first find a place in the humility of the wayside and there, as the multitude crowds by, consecrate my first step, and *beseech*, "JESUS . . . have mercy . . . on *me*." Round me crowds life, and I am part of it, in the midst of it; nor would I flee from it, or its tests, or its duties, its privileges, its mysteries. I would live and pilgrim on as He did; humbly by His gracious gift and acceptance find some place in Life's company so that I may walk with Him,—enter in,—journey on His Way,—in His way.

Life is here: no harder than I make it; and the call to me: a whisper or irresistible,—again the *me*. I cannot travel alone. I cannot escape my fellows. I cannot close my eyes, or my ears, or my heart, or bandage my hands. I *must* live. I *must* walk. I *must* meet the moment's call and challenge, my own or someone else's. I *must* go on and on and on, but I must *live* as I go. Live? . . . "For me to live, is Christ!" Go? . . . "Whose I am, and whom I serve!" Then on through the Gate-way In with Jesus! So into the city we go; and we have a new companion: the gutter-man has become our Brother-of-the-Way.

At the Cross-Roads

✢

✢

MEDITATION

IN THROUGH the open Gate-way moves our company. What curious glances we cast about us as we go! What thoughts, questions, spring to mind. Does something attract my attention, then seem to attack and try to change my will and purpose?—draw me aside?—out of the company?—all so soon! Or one thing or another move me away, and back, and separate me *to* that circle of strangers?

Wake up! On guard! Look up! Look ahead! There where the crowd is thickest *and still going on* is the Master!

But here is something that does call a halt. What is it? The Master has stopped and drawn a little to the side of the way. He is looking about; He glances this way, then that, but never turns to look backward. Now, He is going ahead once more; quiet, definite purpose in every step; face set but looking up,—forward! Yes, He is going right ahead and on and over that road. That's what it was that made the halt, the cross-road. Now I, too, see it; and now I have reached it. Why did *He* stop?

Christ at the Cross-roads!—my Master going up to Jerusalem at the Cross-roads of Jericho. Did it mean anything to Him? Had He not said *where* He was going just the other day? And did He not say *what* would meet Him there? He was so certain of this all. Yes, He paused at the Cross-roads; but He went right on!—to Jerusalem!

To the North, *the way home*; up to Capernaum, "his city," and the quiet of the loved hills and the loveliness of the Lake and its shores. Was there any urge there?

To the South, down along the River, to the wilds and desert and safety of hidden ways, the Dead Sea!— peace, the communion of the solitudes, but the *Dead* Sea. Was there any urge there?

To the East, why that was the way He had come, the way *back*, back over familiar scenes, but *back*! Why turn back? Was there any urge to turn . . . back?

To the West, *ahead,* Jerusalem! and every step o'er rugged way, wild, hard, climb; and every step one nearer to an harder Way. Was there any urge there? He knew that road and all that waited ahead. He knew every step and every stop and every hour and every cost! ". . . Not to do mine own will, but the will of him that sent me" . . . "to finish his work."

He took the road West!

Hear the voice of Jesus calling, "Follow me." Invitation not command. He wants friend, companion; oh, how He wants a friend on *this* road! But He wants something more, too.

So to the Cross-road, pilgrim!

Home and comfort and loveliness and security? That's in one direction; one of the *turns*.

Solitude, away from life and contact and place and duty and privilege and problem and test?—the *Dead Sea*?—the wilderness? That's another.

Turn back? Yes, one can always *turn back*! But can one?

Never! Face the *ahead*! The Great Adventure is always ahead: be it what it may be.

And the Cross-road brings the test, the temptation, the balancing of the personal, the demand to face real and lasting values, the revelation of my inmost being: —(oh, that I may only see myself just as I am, right here, in His Light)—my character, my faith, my love, my confidence, my purpose, my consecration, my promise, my gift. Back of my decision and my first step is all this; but ahead of my decision and my next step . . . walks Jesus. But I can only take one of these roads. I cannot go any way but one if I would follow Him. I cannot follow Him unless I go His way, with Him. I cannot go *my* way, if I want to go with Him, unless *His* way is my way.

Did He not say, "Behold, *we* go . . ."?

I'm across that Cross-road *now*.

The Blocked Road—No Detour!

✛

INSPIRATION : *Read*—St. Luke 19:1-10; Revelation 3:20

✛

MEDITATION

OF COURSE there was a lot of excitement; the street was crowded: for the news had flashed ahead. "That famous teacher is coming. He's on his way to Jerusalem. He has passed the Gate-way In. And think of it! He's just healed blind Bartimaeus!"

Of course they wanted to see Him. They had heard remarkable, sensational, and—breathe it very quietly, —revolutionary things about His teaching and deeds; and now this wonderful thing right here at home— right at *our* Gate-way In! Were not the Great and Holy Men of Israel frowning upon Him? Had He many friends—followers? Oh yes, He had plenty of powerful enemies.

One whispered one thing to another; there a little circle was listening intently to someone else; over there, it looked very much as if a priest were haranguing quite a crowd; all about craning of necks, and pushing out to look down the road: Where is He in all this crowd? Talk about Him everywhere along the way, good and ill; kind word and sneer; whispered longing,—hope, and threat! But the crowd seemed to be unanimous in one thing at least, they all wanted to see Him.

Hear that muffled welling of sound, there in the distance; just a fullness of tone, a deep diapason chord: emotion, voices, excitement, acclaim. It's growing; now it's drowning out the scrape and scruff and scrunch of the traveling throng. No!—no loud huzzahs, but muted Ah's, sighs, intense breathings, rumbling threats, the staccato of comment, a throng beholding the object of its quest.

He comes. He's passing. And then, there under that tree, He stops.

Has Authority blocked the way? Has the crowd gotten out of hand, become a mob to have its will, one way or another?

Much more effectively than by either of these the way has been blocked. A gentle look falls upon the Traveler from the branches of that tree. (That tree is bearing strange fruit. Will it be garnered?) The hope of a heart that feels He has what is needed; that He can give; that He can understand;—just to see Him, look down upon Him, that will be a harvest of peace.

"Zacchaeus, make haste and come down; *for today I must abide at thy house*." Another voice is added to the city's sounds! An impromptu reception, indeed. *Who* is giving it?

And now an host of Why's comes flooding in. Perhaps some of them mine; quite likely! Why the man in the tree for this honor? Why that publican? Why not the Honorable Mr. Justice, or the Right Reverend Mr. Levite, or the rich and powerful Mr. Pharisee? Or, if He wants to slum, why not that wine-bibber there in the rum-shop's door-way? Or, if He's really such a socialist and independent, why not that slinking creature over there, incarnate villany; or that bedizened one of the streets? Yes, Why?

Why stop to visit this fellow? Lose all this time for him? Do I want to have anything to do with that kind of a man? Why meet him socially? or any way? Is he worth anything at all, worth bothering with? Why, he's just . . . a publican! Do I want to associate with him? Would I invite him into my home?—my *pew*? So, why bother to enter his? Do we want *that* sort in *our* Company? Can I share my companionship with him . . . my Companion? *Why this man?*

Answer yourself, Pilgrim! Stop right there in the Road! Look up into that tree bearing newness of life, a new-born man. Look into your own heart and behold the fruitage of your questions, and behold the deadness of *your* self-blocked way. No detour here for me! The man I question blocks my road, and, lo, Another stands at his side! What will I do with the man? What will I do for him? What is he doing to me? What can we do together?

The Other One said, "Make haste . . . I must abide at thy house . . ." And this is why. Because he had ready what the others lacked; because he offered what the others withheld; because he sought what the others only were curious to see; because he longed to claim what somehow he was sure *He* had and that He could give it to him if he would. No wonder Jesus saw him and said to him, "Today I *must* abide at thy house . . ." Would He look at me if He were passing by? . . . would He have any reason to?

A longing heart barricaded the Way.

A longing Heart gladly stopped.

The barricaded way led to the Open Door.

"I will come in to him and will sup with him, and he with me."

The Gate-Way Out

✠

INSPIRATION : St. Luke 9:51—*He steadfastly set his face to go to Jerusalem.*
St. Luke 19:28—*He went before*—
Read—Isaiah 40:28-31; 41:13.

✠

MEDITATION

THEN came the morning after. Another day, and soon the noises of the city, ever increasing,—life awake and on its way once more,—enter that household with call and challenge.

The welcome of that friendly home's harborage glows anew with the new-come light: comfort, peace, companionship; yes, love and mutuality, given, born, grown, these all now there where Jesus is the Guest.

But the noises have their own call! And the stir penetrates;—life's business,—"My Father's business!" So the Guest turns from the hearthstone and faces the door, and the host stands ready to open and speed on His way Him Whom he will ever cherish there.

The door opens to the light. Was it a drab, dull day? Or, did the sun shine? Who knows? But the clouds hung low over the way of the Traveler. No rosy, golden sunrise this to dress the road with fas-

cinating lure and bright appeal; no cheering chirp of
the birds to lighten the heart; no smile to flit along
from flower to flower to beautify, to satisfy; no, not
on that Way.

Out of the door-way and into the street. The call
that gathers the little company, that greets the waiters,
that stirs the laggard, is gentle benediction; is welcome,
"Arise. Come. Follow me." No army at Attention,
to answer the stirring rasp of "Forward!"—this a deeply
consecrated *pilgrimage*. Orison and benediction rise,
and all face forward.

Short distance discovers the open Gate-way Out,
and through it a stretching vista of hard-baked, dusty,
cheerless road, rough and rutted . . . the King's Highway, indeed!—and wild and barren countryside swal-
lowed up in the engulfing chasmed hills. An inspiring
invitation to essay the start! An heartening beginning
to the adventure of the way!—and the open door and
welcoming hearts and peace and quiet and comfort and
friendship . . . all for the turning back! But forward,—"We go up . . ."

Who knows what is ahead? Ah, *He* did!—and nevertheless, still forward: every step sure and certain; face
"steadfastly set", on, to the Gate-way Out; on, through
the Gate-way Out; on, out of the Gate-way Out! The
purpose is present; the way stretches before, be it as
it is; the goal is at the end. But the Traveler, for Him
there is more than obedience, or determination, grim
and dogged; there is inspiration of communion; there

is consecration of oneness with and in the Father's will; there is love of sacrificial spending; there is rapt vision of completion; there is possession of accomplishment. To such an one the comfort of the Presence overcomes the warring way.

And I, also, am passing through the Gate-way Out, for that morning greeting and call has roused me to and hallowed another day. What of the road, Pilgrim, —*your* road? And your objective? Do I have one? And, what of yourself? Lo, I have undertaken to journey with Jesus to Jerusalem!—farthest echo, loud and clear . . . *Jerusalem!* Now, what of this? Ah, earthly, —heavenly,—whither? And what of all that stretches between?

No place for a dreamer of dreams here, or emotional enthusiasms, or cold plan and purpose. My heart must be certain of HIM, and founded surely *in* HIM, and know what is before and what it means to me and demands of me. Face it now, in the drab, dull light, without the glamor of dancing sunbeams;—they will come after a while! A high call to the High Way; but a quiet, serious, demanding call to the Hard Way! "Jesus calls *me* o'er the tumult!" There lies the fellowship of the Traveler. "Strait is the gate . . . narrow is the way . . ."

The road is hard, hard trodden by *world* travelers; rutted by storms; seared by lightning flash of trial and temptation; bleak and cheerless, at times, from sheer loneliness and discouragement; peopled by phantoms;

[17]

and oh, the cross-ways!—and it demands of me the ful-
fillment of purpose, high and holy, the journey of
faith and love and constancy.

For me, here and now, fellowship—(Is not that my
longing?—that I may know him . . . and the fellowship of his sufferings . . . be made conformable unto
him?)—the communion with the Hallowed Presence,
the Fountain of refreshment, inspiration, strength,
encouragement, perseverance, accomplishment, benediction . . ."Well done!" "Not as though I had already attained, either were already perfect: but I follow after, if that I may apprehend that for which also
I am apprehended of Christ Jesus . . . and reaching
forth unto these things which are before, I press toward
the mark for the prize of the high calling of God in
Christ Jesus."

The Company of Jesus

✠

INSPIRATION : *Come unto me, all ye that labor and are heavy laden, and I will give you rest. Take my yoke upon you, and learn of me; for I am meek and lowly in heart: and ye shall find rest unto your souls.*

✠

MEDITATION

NOW isn't that remarkable! I just happened to look about a bit and suddenly I realized a startling thing. Here we are on the High Road, (not of adventure but of great purpose); the Pilgrimage has begun in earnest. And what a busy and crowded road it is: all sorts of travelers are on their way, but not all are going the same way, but all are facing forward, *the way of their choice!*

Now as I looked around, my gaze centered on Him, the Traveler, first of all; and wherever it wandered thereafter it always came back to Him. All centered in Him; all radiated from Him; all seemed to be joined in Him; and far out as one might be, united with Him. Here is the physical association of a traveling company; but that is but a touch: the reality is in the

[19]

invisible bond joining the farthest as well as the closest. But it does not go beyond the Company!—and it does mark the Company uniquely. Crowded as the road is, there is a very definite place of separation, right in this crowd, between the Company of the Traveler and the crowd of the High Road!—and still it is but one great crowd of people traveling.

We are with them, part of it; but certainly not of them. They are with us, all around us,—jostling, pushing, hailing, even walking along and chatting,— but certainly are not of us.

Why is it? What is it? The Traveler? Of course; and *He* makes all the difference in the world!—*all the difference in the world!* He is the center and the difference is the fellowship with Him and the interest in Him and His teaching, and the bond that is forging between Him and us and among us, but never apart from Him.

Like them, we're plodding along the High Road, the *same* road; breathing the same dust; feeling the same scorching heat; stumbling over the same rough places; hearing the same stray birds and seeing (if we do!) the same occasional little wayside flowers; but with what different ears, what different sight!—and faced onward to attainment. But vastly different are the objectives! To them,—? To us, "Jerusalem!" Vastly different the inspiration; vastly different the spirit of the Road. "All the difference in the world!" Objective brings them the common bond of travelers of the way; but the Traveler knits the company into the Fellowship of the Way.

Of course, I'm supposed to have learned and realized all this long ago. But my daily pilgrimage must bring home to me anew the holy treasures and high privileges which fellowship with my Master (the Fellowship of the Way!) opens up to me, not as possibilities but as actualities of my daily life. My way is my life's way, but my life's way can be, must be, journeyed with the Traveler; and that companionship severs me, but does not remove me, from the crowd; there are contacts and relations as real as life makes them, but they are with Him close by.

Companions of the Company

✠

INSPIRATION : *What is that to thee? follow thou me.*

✠

MEDITATION

I SUPPOSE others have been doing the same thing I have been doing. Well, I'll frankly say, I have wanted to see just who came along out of the Gateway Out. Who is in our Company? And I am not interested in comparisons, but I am interested in seeing them with the light of the High Road on their faces, and whether being with the Traveler reveals anything there or other where (I wonder whether any one has looked at mine,—will look at mine to day? Will they see *anything* there?)

There's a van-guard. Guard?—do we need a guard? —on this infested road, with all this company? Surely they will help each other—us. But there is a Vanguard; *He* is going on before, the Leader in the way, "The Captain of our salvation."

Close to Him strides Peter. Seeing him walking so energetically, one feels he would like to rush on ahead; but something restrains him: now an earnest look at the Master, then another off into the distance ahead; he's turning over something in his mind.

Close behind Him walks another; what a difference. Here the step is light but sure, quiet, steady and unhurried; his eyes are set on the clouds above the crags, and there's a wistful, tender, quiet look on his face.

Over there is Andrew. I've grown to love him very dearly since that first day I really saw him when with arm about his shoulders, he brought that little lad and his loaves and fishes to Jesus. He's talking now with that leper the Master healed the other day. There is mutual nodding of heads and confident smiles and, why, they are walking along arm in arm. That's Andrew! and that's fine!—*they* have found something really common to each other.

And that one over there, almost on the edge of the Company, he doesn't seem to want any one to bother him just now; but somehow he just can't keep his eyes away from the Traveler. Hard to get a smile from that brooding one; something is bothering him.

Then, off to the rear, that group of life and smiles and talk and pleasant laughter now and then, the women. One of them, the way she is looking, seems to want to be right up with the men!

And over there is a strange, strange comradeship: a little chap and an awfully ragged fellow. The one is so dignified, but happiness is written all over him, and he doesn't quite know what to make out of the exuberant spirits of his companion. Every few steps he fairly dances along; he is alive with joy; and how they talk, and point, and turn to others about them.

Oh, I have seen all of these folk before! Not one is a stranger; I know them all; and I know something interesting about each one of them and the interesting thing is how and when and *why* they came into the companionship of the Company, when first they joined the Traveler on the Way and determined to journey along. That is one of the bonds that knits me to them: Friends, brethren, companions of the Company,—ah, companions of the experience, of the fellowship, of Jesus:—My impetuous brother, my dreaming brother, my brooding, resentful brother; my friend who was comforted, my brother who was encouraged, my sister who was healed, my companion who was rescued: wiped away tears, mended hearts, rebuilt lives, new-born purposes,—all are there, and more!—and humbly, let me say, So am I.

The Magnet,—the Welcome; the Cleansing,—the Union; the Fellowship, Jesus' harvest of lives: He has surrounded Himself with new-born men; He is traveling for them, with them, the Road of the Rebuilding of Lives.

Any One Missing?

✦

INSPIRATION : *From that time many of his disciples went back, and walked no more with him.*

Read—St. Mark 10:17-22.

✦

MEDITATION

OUR Company has been moving forward steadily. The rough road is getting rougher; the hills have grown into rugged cliffs; our way seems to be leading into that fearsome, yawning maw in the mountains just ahead; how dark and forbidding—with its frowning desire to draw us in and engulf us! Our little Company draws closer together,—yes, nearer to *Him*. Are we seeking protection?—from Him? Our Company seems to be growing more solid, more compact, there's a cohesion we did not have before; and now we are presenting quite a strong front. Yes, our "strongest" are up there beside Him, and here and there along the sides others, and at the rear others, wakeful, watchful, sturdy, ready men. All eyes are front! Danger ahead? Who knows? The Adventure of the Unknown and the Unexpected may be right around the corner.

Thus drawn closely together I can see our Company as it is; and pretty well, too, one catches the spirit and the mental strength and weakness. No better time than this to see oneself as one is in the face of danger and in the challenge to courage.

But there is something more. One sees definitely who is here. Is it because one is merely curious to see, or is taking account of the "forces" we have, or on whom we can rely? Is any one missing? From *this* Company? Did some one fail to start this morning? Was some one left behind in Jericho? Did any one drop out along the road?—"fall by the wayside?" Did any one turn back because of the danger ahead? That *has* happened, more than once; and sometimes right at the time of greatest need!

Too often one thinks of the challenge to one's spiritual undertaking from the physical side, from the purely personal, from the equipment of desire and intention and not from the depth of the trial and the test of every part there is to me and what I need to meet it, measure up to it, battle with it, and please God, conquer it, too, *besides what I have* with which to meet it. Too often I'll face forward and emotion will cry out, "Yes, I'll go." "I'll do!" and heart's eye will vision *Him* and what I *call* faith will start me off, but—! Something far greater is needed than this. Fellowship with the Traveler; inspiration to answer the call; faith to find and know and own Him, the reality of personal fellowship; confidence, the well-spring of endeavor; courage, the twin of facing forward; trust, the panoply spread over by Him Who travels along; love, the spender of self in Him and for Him. This all means pretty much the giving over of one's *whole* self to Him and His Companionship; doesn't it? Well, why not? He has given Himself for me,—to me. And all He offers to me, what of that? And what of the enabling inspiration of the fellowship,—proceeds, and I draw, from Him; proceeds, and I draw, from those who *have* drawn from Him? Lacking these every shadow holds a fear, every corner brings a chill; and the engulfing way is faced with half-heart that means trembling and defeat.

Never-Start, Turn-Back and Drop-Out are missing.

The Ravine of the Awesome Test

✤

INSPIRATION : *Yea, though I walk through the valley of the shadow of death, I will
fear no evil: for thou art with me;
thy rod and thy staff they comfort
me.*

✤

MEDITATION

THERE are two things about this crisis in the Company's journey that are remarkable, and the second is only because there is a first.

That road never was pleasant to travel, and no one
ever thought it an easy way, and every one knew it
was infested with dangers. Some things could be fore-
seen and prepared for; others came unawares. Woe
to those unprepared!

The Ravine of the Awesome Test is here! Our little
Company has closed in. All eyes now forward. The
morale is good. What's ahead? Certainly there is
trepidation: who does not feel the challenge of the
unknown, the lurking thing? That does not mean
cowardly fear necessarily; brave men feel fear too.
One goes forward nevertheless, so, too, our footsteps,
and they are not dragging either. For JESUS is here!

What confidence His presence instills! What courage! . . . ("I can do all things through Christ who strengtheneth me!") *With us;* with me, among the all of us. *For* us all, and for me, too.

One does not stop to question or even think about Him or seek to discover how He feels, why, *of course,* to Him there is no other way! The high purpose of self-giving can go but one way, on and through!— not on and around but *on and through!* Self-less service,—the consecration of self to the needs of others, the winning of others to the consecration of self-giving, does not spend itself in the face of minor issues but immolates its devotion in singleness of purpose.

Courage or consecration? Was it courage because of consecration, or consecration born of courage? And the calm, untroubled, steady onward going, on, on, down, in,—ever forward!—the Traveler is here and journeying on! Fear? Why, He is journeying on! And He has the inspiration that makes fear afraid and slink away,—that casts it away. One of the Company wrote afterward, "Perfect love casteth out fear"; —remember? He has that perfect love, and like a peaceful shower it is falling over every heart in the Company ("Thy rod and thy staff, they comfort me!") That is the *other* thing this crisis discloses: Stout hearts *because of Stout Heart*; forward going because He is going forward: the devotion, the will, the sacrifice, the meeting,—His, ours, *mine,* not emotional imitation or mere reflection of example, but born of His presence, inspired by His calm, consecrated purpose.

And so One passes it on to others, and others pass it on to each other; and in that *union* of high love and faith and trust, on, down, in! We'll come through *with Him*! All show it, this Glorious Company of Jesus! . . . But what would we be,—what would we do, without *Him*?

A Place . . . for Me

✛

INSPIRATION : *This man receiveth sinners. . . .*

> *. . . We have fellowship one with another, and the blood of Jesus Christ his Son cleanseth us from all sin.*

✛

MEDITATION

THERE has been many a kindly greeting, cheery word and smile, touch of welcome and friendly help since I found a place in this blessed Company. There's a warmth and a reality and an assurance of acceptance, the equal of which I have never found anywhere else. Not only have I been made to feel welcome, but that I really *belong*, that I am a part of the Company. And then the interest, well, that has always been the sort that concerned, and concerned itself about, *my good*.

But the kindest of all, and the smile that reached my heart, and the word that stirred my soul, and the hand that drew me in, . . . was *His*. Welcome and *welcome*, indeed!—to *me*! He made me feel that He wanted me; and how I realized that I needed, wanted, must have and be with Him!

So I came. And I carried what I brought when that day came that will ever mark my welcome there before Him, and when my heart said, "Stay." And when I stayed, lo, what I had brought was no longer mine own. There was the look that read my heart; there was the life that probed into the depths of mine; there was the word that crashed through the deafness of my false will; there was the call to holiness that flashed its light over my shadowed way; and I saw myself as I was, in all my weakness and sin. Could there be any thing worth His while in such as me? How could He possibly want *me*? Could He have a place for me?

Then came the dawn suffusing a golden longing for the hope and beauty of holiness and purity, and the urge within to go to Him, a sudden purpose to go just as I was and carry what I brought *to Him*, open my very soul to Him, tell Him all: my sin, my need, my utter worthlessness, and yet, my hope, my plea, my claim on His *apparent* willingness to listen to me. There was He, standing, waiting, looking right at me, compelling me . . . to come . . . or to go! Compelling me *to go*? Ah, no, never! But to decide my going myself. And I knew right then that if I would come I would be welcome; that He would have a place for me.

A place of the old things left behind;
　　of the new things found;

of listening and learning;
of waiting and following;
of surrendering myself and finding Him;
of Him and His, who become mine and whose I
become:
of learning love and loving service;
of life in Him,—for Him;
of traveling along,—with Him and His.
A place found . . . given to me.

Something Decidedly Wrong

✣

INSPIRATION : *Lord, that I may receive my sight.*

✣

MEDITATION

SOMETHING went decidedly wrong on my journey yesterday, and thinking it over I realize I have no one to blame for it except myself and possess not so much as a shadow of an excuse. Now, today, there is a great deal more blame that concerns me: shame and sorrow, and a hunger to see things as I should and to do the things I should; these possess me now.

The stress of circumstances, suppressed feelings, one thing and another that put me "on edge,"—all of these, not in extenuation, but rather as realization that when I am so keyed up or down, or "temperamental," or ab- or sub-normal, then is the time I am on trial, the *me* and what I am professing, and just when the test of the vitality of my religion, my *Jesus-union*, is put to the mark *in me*!

I was critical. I began to look around at others and compared them with myself; oh, no, of course not to my injury! I scoffed at their weaknesses, never seeing that I was worse than weak. I had already surrendered my fight!

[34]

I was proud. I was puffed up over the way *I* was looking ahead, and how keen I was to get right into the midst of the crisis and meet whatever was there. I'd show them what bravery was and how to face the issue!

I was consumed with self-importance. I did not want to stay *back* in *my* place; I wanted to be *up front* in some one else's place. Couldn't they see how much *I* was needed there, and all *I* could do, and how well *I* could do it,—so much better than some who were there? This, never realizing, not for a moment, that I had not yet even stood the tests which make the forefront guards dependable.

I looked down on my fellow-travelers. What, that *leper* here beside me! Why are such as he allowed to join our company? And that *publican*; and that low fellow over there: I did not want to have anything to do with such people. And really, what good are they? Why so much as notice them? But I did, in *that* way!

All this, and more. Oh, I was utterly out of tune and like a peevish, mean-spirited child I began to sulk. I'd show them. I drew away from every one; would not talk to them; rebuffed them; snapped at whoever talked to me. My self-centered self-importance made me smaller and smaller with every step. Oh, barren conceit and pride! Oh, shallow soul,—seed fallen on the rock!

So I kept pushing away and back. I'd drop out

of this crowd, if this was all they were going to make of me. And I came to the last, last row. Involuntarily my glance flashed along its front, and, self-centered though I was, I realized that every last row man was a disciple tested and tried! Here a moment's shame for what I had resolved to do kept me from dropping aside with some trite excuse on my lips,— *that* I could mumble! Resentfully I dragged along near them, something stirring within me. What a story each one of these men could tell, and here they were on the *back* row! I looked ahead to the *front* row; curious to compare; and was startled not to find the Traveler there. My eye flashed about until I found Him. He was walking in and out among the company; talking to this one; smile here; word there; kindly touch to another. I knew instantly *He* was encouraging, ministering the assurance of His Presence. And suddenly He looked at me! I'll never forget that reading, asking look. He looked at me and I saw myself:—myself and Him.

Realization

✠

INSPIRATION : *And the Lord turned and looked upon . . . Peter.*

And when he thought thereon, he wept.

I said, I will confess my transgression unto the Lord; and thou forgavest the iniquity of my sin.

✠

MEDITATION

THE first thing that came home to me under that precious look was that I had failed Him, not well-nigh, but *that I had utterly failed Him.* I had given over. I had never thought of Him. I had been thinking of myself even when I had thought of others, but never of Him; and He had never been out of my sight; no, not for a second. I was barren ground indeed,—a selfish heart.

What a traitor! There is no other word for it; no gentle word; no excusing word. Bald, hard, undeniable fact, a traitor. My heart had not pulsed one loyal beat, high-strung with self-assured enthusiasm though it had been, "*Me* to the front or nowhere!"—and suddenly I realized I had been bound full-speed for the

"Nowhere." And where is that but where I am not with Him?

Fight battles for Him? What good am I for any need, any crisis, when the test of the preparation, even before I'd ever come face to face with the great issue, found me so utterly routed and worthless and retreating to surrender to the enemy,—*His* enemy?

Shame! Surely! Oh, that *now* I could find a way-off place to hide my one-time proud, self-assertive self-importance; and from afar look on Him and humbly plead to His all-hearing heart to be forgiven. Perhaps there, in the humble place I might be permitted still to walk along,—perhaps. And, even though I did not deserve it, perhaps I might follow along with the man who had been a leper, and learn the real bravery of humility, the real victory of cleansed and purified and reborn self; and when the need would come, *do*!—yes, do what I could.

Hope followed; waking resolutions; a strength of purpose growing, purified; a warmth in my heart; a different vision of my fellow travelers at whom I'd sneered, on whom I had looked down. After all they were of His choosing, His receiving. I was less than the least; worse than the worst;—a traitor to the Traveler, a turn-back, a self-lover, a worldling, an enemy. How little of all I'd heard Him say; how little of all I'd seen Him live; how little of Himself had become part of me. How much there was to lose of me and to find and own of Him!

Another look came to me. This time tender, kind, comforting, encouraging, accepting! I had found my place and accepted it; and He had found and forgiven and kept me;—*this I knew!*

It Might Have Happened Here

✛

INSPIRATION : *Bear ye one another's burdens, and so fulfil the law of Christ.*
Read—ROMANS 12:9ff.

✛

MEDITATION

A HAND was laid on my arm. Some one was drawing me back to walk beside him: a friendly, brotherly touch, just at the right time. After *that* look, this; how warm my heart felt now. A glance showed me Andrew, and he had made room for me to walk beside him in the *last* row, beside him, one of the rear-guard. Still at the other side walked the man who had been a leper. Remember? I did; and there was a generous smile of greeting from him too. No longer, —oh, thankfully I felt it, and yet, still with the sense of shame,—did I look on him as I had. I was happy to smile back. Yes, I would be glad to walk beside *him*. He was in the rear-guard, too.

But that was not all. Very quietly a voice spoke to me.

"Brother, don't you remember what the Master said the other day; how much we need each other, how much we can be to, and can help, each other, whoever we are? Open your eyes. Look about. *It might have happened here!"*

My eyes traveled about: frowning cliffs, high, craggy, perilous; down here in the half-light, the rough road: we were in the depths of that awesome place. Yes, it might have happened here; just the place for such a thing. I did not need to be told any more. It all came back to me: the man going down from Jerusalem to Jericho and how in just such a forsaken, terrifying place, as this, traveling alone, he fell among thieves. I could see him: attacked, brutally beaten, thrown to the roadside and left there a pitiful bit of thrown-away life, the object of his fellowman's desire!—his possessions, precious, but his life, cheap; himself of no interest save for what he had and what they could *take from* him;—stripped, wounded, bleeding, aching; the clock running down,—darker, darker,—*alone* in such a forsaken, sunless place as this,—alone with his fellowman's gift to him, pain, misery! Oh, for a bit of light, a gentle breeze, a drop of water,—yes, even a fellowman! The *priest*, minister of Jehovah's mercy, mediator in sacrifice and blessing, dispenser of the healing loving kindness,—the *Levite*, servant of the Presence, singer of Jehovah's goodness, beneficiary of his brethren's constant giving,—these see *him*, look upon him with varying emotions, and hurry, hurry on *their* way.

Oh, woe to me, who looked on my own fellows with a vision such as this, who never saw their need of me, who beheld the *without* and was blind to the *within*, who judged the external in my own standards, —valueless,—and threw away the riches of a soul!

And why? Because I could not see what I was not ready to give. I could see what I was ready to condemn. So did the priest and the Levite. They condemned the *thieves!*—but ——!

Heap up the names for the ignominious, *godless,* retreat from opportunity and privilege; scoff at such profession of religion and such exponents of piety and morality; pity the self-centered, near-sighted "holiness" that recognizes and condemns a wrong with vision blurred to help and cure; this all crowds on *me* and condemns *my selfish revision* of the Master's golden service rule; and bows me down in shame as I vision the gentle, brotherly, practical salvaging and protection of the Samaritan. Oh, Master!

Time to remember whither I am traveling! "Who shall ascend into the Hill of the Lord: or who shall stand in His Holy Place?"

Oh, Master give me the heart, the religion of *Thy* Samaritan.

A Resting Place

✦

INSPIRATION : *This is the rest wherewith ye may*
cause the weary to rest, and this is
the refreshing . . .
His resting-place shall be glorious.

✦

MEDITATION

WE HAVE moved steadily onward, and I have
been thinking as we journeyed. Suddenly I realized that the light is growing stronger. I can see
things more plainly, the shadows are resolving into
familiar objects; the way before is quite plain,—only
behind me is the dark! The sun shines down on us
again; our spirits rise, hearts are opening. Now the
tense quiet of our Company gives place to a growing
volume of voices: perhaps the interchange of feelings,
emotions, experiences. Best for me to try and leave
mine back there in the dark, and look ahead,—"forgetting the things that are behind . . . press on to
the goal . . ."

The way is broadening; even the craggy cliffs seem
to be in retreat before our buoyant host. Now a
glimpse of open countryside ahead. How welcome that
touch of green, sun-faded though it be. We're leav-

ing the darksome place; but I shall carry the memory and the lesson, even to the green fields!

Over there a gentle slope, a bit of welcome shade, a refreshing little rill; the Master is leading the way and our little Company comes to the moment's rest at His kindly invitation, circling about Him, sinking down on the grass, hearts ready to listen.

So every day along the Highway brings its chance and change; its purpose and interruption; its test and struggle; its defeat and realization; its reawakening and resolution; its harvest of one's own sowing or slackness. Rest comes,—not at last, ah, no; but as benediction for recuperation, for greater purpose, for perseverance. And such moments are hallowed; consecrated to closest companying with Him,—even alone with Him . . . in the midst of a crowd.

Exclusion of the world; exclusion from the world; inclusion of the Master; and the resting place is the school of enrichment to him that sits at the Master's feet. Thus shall I learn discipleship.

At the Wayside
Learning Discipleship

✛

INSPIRATION : *The high calling of God in Christ Jesus . . .*

✛

MEDITATION

THE Resting Place at the Wayside is a good place to go to school. True rest is not inertia but recreation, *re*creation, a refreshment built of assimilated benefits. One visions all that is before:—imagination is always playing with the romance of the What-may-be;—oh, *this* Road; and to *where* the King's Highway leads! This I have determined to travel with Him. He knows *His* possibilities; He knows *His* equipment and reserves;—do I know mine? or the lack of them? Well that He does for me? So the school hour of remembrance here at the Wayside on the King's Highway.

Discipleship,—"So shall ye be my disciples . . ." How little one needs to waken the heart to what one has heard and knows when it is *His* voice that speaks. How glibly the lesson is recited; but how little or poorly it has been digested and assimilated and become part and parcel of one's self,—*become one's self.*

Discipleship is never one-sided,—His call and teaching, or my acceptance and listening. There are "His's" and "my's", but the possessive pronoun is really "ours", and it always is *possessive*, this pronoun of discipleship.

Discipleship is fellowship: not receptivity on one side only, for He is willing to receive from the disciple as well as to give to him that receives from Him; not inter-change, oh no,—nor mere mutuality of objective and purpose. There is relation here, but objective and purpose are of Master and learner; and only after the learner *has* learned and continues to learn, only then do his objective and purpose approach the Master's and begin to measure up to them!

Discipleship is of the day of life: an occupation within one's occupation; an ideal which becomes the daily reality; a practice that becomes living; a spiritual inspiration which lives in actualities, visualizes itself in the facts of life.

Discipleship is transplanting and translating the heavenly into the realm of the earthly: endless in possibilities though starting in the seed germ of the hardly recognized and, to the world, undesired; fabulous in treasures, poverty to the world, but overshadowing the gold and glitter with the purity and splendor of the Pearl of Great Price.

Discipleship is investment: divine in its inception and spending; divine in its generosity and beneficence; divine in its earning and in its plan of endless reinvestment; divine in its trust.

Discipleship is a new kind of declaration of independence: a proclamation and rebellion against, and renunciation of, sin, flesh, and devil's sway;

A new declaration of new-found manhood, inspired by the Supremest Manhood!

A new declaration of new values;

A new declaration of new objectives;

A new declaration to the world of a new thing and a new term—the value of a soul;

A new invitation to this old world's ears and ways, and a challenging cry to recognition by the aching, hungering void of need and longing aspiration;

An allegiance, a fellowship, a following, a oneness and completion described only in its own terms; known only to its initiates; consummated only in the individual decision, acceptance, surrender, and loving obedience.

"Learn of me . . ." Ah, in Him, this all is revealed,—in the Jesus of the Wayside and of the Highway,—of the Home and of the Temple,—of the Manger and of the Cross,—of the Tomb and of the Tongues of Flame! "Learn of me . . ." and for me . . . "if any man would come after me . . ." His call to me, "Follow!"

Learning Discipleship
Decision

✠

INSPIRATION : . . . *And counteth the cost, whether he have sufficient to finish it . . .*

✠

MEDITATION

HERE at the Wayside with the vista of grim reality; the foreboding of the coming days and
events; the deep, oppressive gloom of man's inhuman-
ity, self-will, false valuing, treachery; the tragedy of
rejection; with the Cross looming ahead like an angry-
clouded tempest of wrath and destruction,—here, with
this,—sensing it all, balancing its lessons, is a time of
times to learn discipleship in its true values and true
demands.

As the Traveler speaks to us of discipleship, recall
the comers to the master. One might even think of
Him reminding us of them: of the many who came,
were interested to varying degrees, listened enraptured,
nodded affirmation, accepted the benefits,—and did not
stay!

Of the Young Man, so full of enthusiasm, so sure
of his own spiritual value, so satisfied with his obedience to religion's requirements, so pious in rite and

ceremony, so *legally* righteous,—"All this have I kept from my youth . . ." Poor fellow he had *kept* it,— he hadn't put it into circulation! The Divine Physician prescribes the remedy: "One thing thou lackest . . ." the prescription of *active, personal expenditure:* "Go!— Sell!—Give!—Come!—Follow!" "ALL"—"ME"! He, too, went away.

Of the hungry multitude that followed and lingered; that listened and only partly learned; fanned to enthusiasm because of the cure of ills temporal and physical; reaching for the ideals of aspiration but falling to the level of the carnal; like every mob, selfish, self-seeking; looking for the easy way and for some one else to carry the responsibility,—*theirs!*—to think for them; to provide for them; and disappointed and disillusioned at the final realization of responsibility thrown home. "These have no root . . ." But, "Blessed are they that *hunger and thirst after righteousness*, for they shall be filled."

Then the Three in the Gospel, two of whom voluntarily assert their purpose to follow, one invited to by the Master. The first had to learn and realize the cost it meant to him; the second instantly qualified his determination and willingness; the third had not reached the point of great and instant valuation and response. All,—take all,—give all. All of Him: all of me! No half way; no hang-back; no double way; no qualifications;—with . . . against; gathering, . . . scattering; *or* not *and.*

The Cross-roads of Discipleship,—it is reached only once,—the first time!

Hand to the plough and look back,—

Realization

He has what I need

He has what I want

Valuation

He offers that to me

He calls to me

Renunciation

In these hours again, the echoing Voice down the valley of time:—

Counteth the cost

Doth not forsake

Deny himself

Take up his cross

Daily

Follow . . . ME

It rests with *me*, that decision; as I see Him; as I hear His words; as my soul reacts to His all; as my life responds, my will, my faith, as I deny or glorify myself. It rests with me.

Learning Discipleship
Determination

✝

INSPIRATION : *Where shall wisdom be found?*
Behold, the fear of the Lord, that
is wisdom; and to depart from evil
that is understanding.
That I may know him . . .

✝

MEDITATION

*A*ND *he saith unto them, But whom say ye that I
am?*

This, after all, is the very center of things: His challenging question. Nor is it wholly a matter of saying,
admission, confession. There is a shorter or longer
reach back of it and the far road of eternity stretching
onward from it.

*And Peter answereth and saith unto him, Thou art
the Christ.*

Yes, Master, here at your feet, at the Wayside on
the King's Highway. You ask me that!—and I *must*
answer! *I* must! No, not words alone. Once more,—
not words alone!

Discipleship presents this reality, and faces one with
it. One must face it, meet it, and dispose of it,—and

[51]

there are two ways of disposing of it!—This reality: Who is,—What is,—Why is,—the Master?

And every angle of approach, and every contact, is a line direct to me and a return direct from me. The realities of His possessions that He would make mine own have been subjected to, and have stood the tests of, my needs and of my making:—His glorious love, His transcendent ALL,—(Oh, how this Highway leads, reminds, and promises!) "This have I done for thee," —His offer, His desire to have, to welcome, to trust, to rely on, to possess,—me!

"What shall a man give in exchange for his soul?" His heritage of the victory of the Cross? His garnering to come through the triumph of the Tomb? What will I give in exchange for that?

Will I give away the defeated things? Will I give away the passing things? Will I give away the separating things? Will I give away the destroying things? Will I give away the worthless things?—the will that defeats; the flesh that sins; the doubt that kills; the desires that enslave; the purposes that darken; the selfishness that banishes? What will I give? *I?*—What, that *He* will graciously consider and accept as a *treasure to Himself?* What will I give—*in exchange;* —yes, to receive for my giving something instead; to *receive,*—possess,—become my very own;—for my soul? To give *Him* my soul? My very self.

"Here, Lord, I give myself away"—to Thee—
" 'Tis all that I can do."

Learning Discipleship
The Discipline of the Commonplace

INSPIRATION : *Teach us to number our days, that we may apply our hearts unto wisdom.*

Show me thy ways, O Lord: teach me thy paths.

Day by day, we magnify thee.

Vouchsafe, O Lord, to keep us this day without sin.

MEDITATION

BUT,—yes, *BUT!* as I listen to the Master and learn the lessons of discipline, let me be sure to come to definite realities. He wants me, too; He wants nothing else. He does not want over-enthusiasm, nor rash decision, nor sharply sudden forward going. He wants definite, deliberate realization of responsibility:—analyze this, "response-ability"— ability to meet and answer, measure up to, the test!

I may set myself for the tests and trials that I know are sure to come with somewhat of the heroic spirit of martyrdom. Fatalism?—or even pessimism? Do I admit such a thing there? Hardly; rather that I'm all set for the hard tests; I'm going about expecting them; and I know I *have* to meet them and bear them, so I'll carry them. O, Pilgrim, what a sorry fellow you are then! What a mournful, burdensome dole you make out of your life! How you misread your privilege! You say, Well, call it *Christian* pessimism. Do you dare to? Is there such a *thing* as that? That is a sad and serious mistake and not learning the lesson of the discipline of discipleship. Here's the name for what you must have,—*The Pilgrim's Preparedness,* and it is the result of His lessons learned, the real outcome of His disciplining; *readiness,* not of expectation, but for meeting the test when it does come.

Learn the *result* of discipline. This is to be beneficial, salutary, constructive; a preparation and equipment for eventualities; a building of character; development of allegiance, of loyalty, faith, trust; the strengthening and consecration of will; the mellowing and growth of heart. The Master wants me to learn that the Divine purpose of discipline is *not* punishment or a mere testing of my character or to see how much dependence can be placed in me: all these have a place, but not primary!—but it is the purging of the dross, the refining of the gold, the bringing out in me through this the vital things for life and eternity.

Now this is fine for the big things,—and the big tests come too,—oh, how they sift me to the marrow! But is my discipleship built only of mountain tops and deep ravines? Is it only the extraordinary, the severe,

the great crises? What of the quiet, open, sun-lit road?
—my daily life?—the common things of the common
day? The Master wants me to know *now* as I linger
here with Him at the Wayside on the King's Highway
that there *is but one* Good Friday!—*but* how many
"every days" He journeys through before *that day*
comes!—and His "every days" were not easy days!

So I must realize and face and appropriate and be
benefited by the discipline of the commonplace. Daily
issues, relationships, occupation, personal habits, concerns, purposes, desires and attitudes: all these and
more,—*every one of them,* sooner or later,—and when
not?—are disciplining me for Him; for am I not living my *now* for Him as well as the high moment? Am
I not living for Him when I am with my companions
as well as when I am alone in the dark valley? Am
I not living for Him and with Him when I am going
about the concerns of my daily life as well as when
some sudden and unusual stroke calls a halt and
throws all awry and demands an immediate proof of
the hope that is in me.

Between "Good Morning" with its well started day
of sunshine or cloud and "Good Night" with its fold-
ing away in the benediction of rest, every minute is
schooltime for me. Oh, harvest, Pilgrim, the lessons
of the discipline of the commonplace of the common
day.

Learning Discipleship
Dependence

✛

INSPIRATION : *I am the vine, ye are the branches.*
As the branch cannot bear fruit of
itself, except it abide in the vine; no
more can ye, except ye abide in me.

That they all may be one; as thou,
Father, art in me, and I in thee, that
they also may be one in us . . .

✛

MEDITATION

THE paradox of losing one's life to find it, of losing one's self to find it, does not remain a paradox
but becomes a realized reality in the blessed process of
growth in discipleship. One may endeavor to translate
this into matter of fact expression and try to describe
it,—even to oneself;—but, after all, it is not a matter
of expressing it but of *realizing* it, of knowing one *has*
found *the* life, that one has found one's self, and of
recognizing one's self 'mid old realities in new relationships and new and transcending responsibilities.
And then I am ready to ask myself: Did *you* really find
that light?—did *you* really find your self?—did
not *He* find them for you and give them to you?

Expressing it all, will follow then; cannot help but follow; *must* follow; but it will be in much more than words! It will be in a further realization: the fulness and completeness and absolute necessity of my union with my Master,—my dependence upon Him.

I tarry here at the Wayside with the Traveler and vision all that stretches ahead for Him. Losing Himself?—losing *His* life?—to find what *in all that*? To build a Life and a Kingdom—in me, for one!—and to knit me to Himself in the never to be loosed bond of discipleship that He is forging minute by minute about me.

I come to Him;—He welcomes me.

I bring Him my need;—He meets it.

I listen to Him;—He heartens me.

I go with Him;—He encourages me.

I espouse Him;—He accepts me.

I open my heart to Him;—He fills it.

I give Him my life;—He gives me His.

I adventure His service;—His presence accompanies me.

I give Him my poverty;—He enriches me.

I offer Him my weakness;—He strengthens me.

I surrender my will to Him;—He abides with me.

I depend on Him;—He lives in me.

And here is roused in me the *response*,—activities. Discipleship isn't all teaching and listening. Oh, no, not by any means; there's a turn: Come allegiance and loyalties; service and actions; demand and expenditures; testimony and fruitages; and when need be, to stand and withstand . . . "He that is not with me is against me; he that gathereth not with me scattereth." Tense, *intense* ACTIVITY, the *LIFE*!

Oh, but the breath, the strength, the will, the heart, the consecration? Have I not heard, and do I not know, full well, that "with might of *mine* naught can be done"? Is not this very power in me, new found through loss, the reality of union,—Life? And what did He say to me? "I am the Life." Discipleship becomes fellowship. No more can I, except I abide in Him; no more can I bring the fruitage for His glory's harvesting except He abide in me. Fellowhip becomes partnership, and its realization brings home to me the full need of my dependence upon Him in all things, at all times.

Learning Discipleship
Devotion

✙

INSPIRATION : *When ye pray . . .*
Verily, verily, I say unto you?
Whatsoever ye shall ask the Father
in my name, he will give it you.
Rejoice evermore.
Pray without ceasing.
In every thing give thanks.
The Great Example: St. John 17.

✙

MEDITATION

GO INTO thy closet. Shut to the door. And pray
. . .

Here is the handmaiden of realized dependence and
the unfailing means to certain dependability.

As I sit here at the Wayside near the Master and
listen to Him as He builds for me step by step the life
of discipleship, I go back over the Way and vision these
steps in the memories of realities. Seeing the development in myself or in others I love in the actualities of
building of character and union and allegiance and
service,—of redeemed and remade lives,—brings a
warmth of quiet satisfaction. Ah, no; not self-satis-

faction or pride in accomplishment; simply the happy glowing contentment that only comes when one knows that one is His.

How much He has done for, given to, showered upon me! But how little actually of all I wanted to give . . . and can!—have I given Him. There never was any lack on His part, or withholding, or restraint, or refusal; freely, bounteously given,—rich, running over!

I have experienced this under many circumstances:— When many have been present, I never failed to receive my peculiarly needed share; or few, the same; as we journeyed or when we rested; in the city or in some home; but the moments that stand out above all others are those *when I was alone with Him.* Oh, the intimacies of such moments,—"The Love of Jesus, what it is, none but His loved ones know"—benign, tender forgiveness, acceptance; sympathetic, quiet, personal, interested helpfulness; magnetic, curative, soul-healing ministry, uniquely for me; full enfolding and unfolding communion; strengthening, enriching, equipping inspiration;—the Master and I.

And so He leads me to the quiet hours of personal communion. His own example is ever before me: the quiet, *alone,* place, where He found it; where He made it: before dawn, or at midday; mountain-side or wilderness; synagogue or flower covered field; life filled street or hidden fireside; every place, every contact, in His example of approach and communion with His Father. And did *He* need? He surely sought and found, and, oh, how His face shone with the finding, and how His heart spent the found treasure!

So find thy "closet," Pilgrim, or carry it with thee, or build thee one!—oh, yes, *all along the way.* "Shut to thy door"; yes, in the hurly burly; in the common things; or in the vaulted reach of hidden moments alone,—and commune.   Thy needs:—

> Thyself for His discipleship;
> the bond that must be kept living;
> the fervor that must be kept warm;
> the faith that must be kept sure;
> the love that must be kept profligate;
> the zeal that must be kept burning;
> the courage that must be kept unfailing.

Ah, no; there is no magic here; but quiet, tender hours of communion, alone with Him, listening with open ears and open heart; meditation, following the guide, drinking in the Spirit; adoration, the outpouring of the meed of praise and love; prayer, for thyself, thy faithfulness, thy usefulness, the hunger of ingathering, the rapture of victory for Him.

Build thee a closet everywhere, and live with Him, in Him, for Him, for thy sake, the hidden life of devotion.

Learning Discipleship Dependability

✠

INSPIRATION : . . . *Sleepest thou? couldest not thou watch one hour? Give an account of thy stewardship . . .*

✠

MEDITATION

THERE is a winnowing and purifying, as by the cleansing fire of Divine Sacrifice, in the realization of all this Highway leads to,—which all *is for me*; but there is exaltation in the realization of the heirship, of the testament, of the committed trust, of the entrusted administration, of the reliance, *the gift of the Giver of all to me;* an exaltation born of realized, profoundly realized, unworthiness, weakness, insufficiency, high and holy resolve, and implicit dependence upon promised Presence and aid.

Were one to view the future of active discipleship as one looks into the *Ahead* this day from the Wayside here, and there loomed ahead of *me* and *for* me as surely and definitely and searchingly my future as He previsions His own, what a complex would crash in on me; what a wreck of panic stricken fearfulness would engulf me! But it is not fear but the exaltation of hopeful usefulness, of loving spending that rises from my soul to answer His gracious acceptance of me, to respond to the committed mission and to go forward for Him, just as I am, as He has accepted me, as He will make me fit, to administer the trust at least faithfully.

That the Treasure of His Victory is given me to administer and to spend on and for others,—to *me* of all men!—must force me to my knees before Him in completest humility. To *stand* before Him Who died to give to me that I might have and have to give, is the presumption of self-reliance that will meet no test, that reveals dependence misplaced.

That He in the royalty of His abiding Victory, in all the power of His Cross, in all the never dying glory of His Tomb, reaches into my life to call me to this heritage; that He deigns to glance at me,—transcending assurance;—that He loves me, has given Himself to me, wants me; that this all is guarantee that *this is so*, and that to me He gives that I may have and, I say again, have to give to others in His Name, —oh, the crown of full, complete consecration! And I am to be His feet to go; and His voice to speak:— to invite, to welcome, to encourage, to comfort, to bless; and His hands to give; and His heart to love! Oh, Divine trust!—"the foolishness of God"—depending on me?

Discipleship is growing, expanding, increasing life in the Way, the Truth and the Life. Discipleship is spent in the doing and the meeting, with the best one has just as one is, but confident of the doing and the meeting *together*. Discipleship is "Lord, here am I send me"; the surrender accepted to be strengthened for His accomplishment. I think of the joy and not of the woe at the end; of the "Well done" and not of the "Take from him that he hath." For, "for me to live" is "that I may be found in him." I think not whether I am dependable or not, nor of loyalty or failure, simply, *only*, of the joy of accepting and accomplishing His will.

Learning Discipleship
Destination

✠

INSPIRATION : . . . *Reaching forth unto those*
things which are before, I press to-
ward the mark for the prize of the
high calling of God in Christ Jesus.
For . . . your life is hid with
Christ in God.
That where I am, there ye may be
also.

✠

MEDITATION

AND here at the Wayside I must learn too, that the
Traveler is going Home. The King's Highway
has an end, but it is not at the Cross-crowned Hill.
This is but a stopping place forced by man and sur-
mounted by our heroic Warrior. Victorious in defeat?
Defeating His victors? Nor is it in the Valley cradling
the Tomb. This is but a resting place devised by man,
—the shadow-land of buried hopes; the hiding place
of torn hearts; the secret temple of love's sacrifice,
tears; the grave of man's Why?—a couch where *He*
could not rest long or be holden; for was He not
eager to travel on?—and so rises all-glorious from His

rest. Nor does the Highway end on the Hill of Farewell where loving hearts face the parting, the while gazing into the Beyond. Destination? The King's Highway ends only at the Sapphire Throne, and there the Son has come Home.

Oh, what an hard, hard way He traveled to There; and how He traveled! What a vast reach from There down to Here. What astounding, tremendous poles of difference: the vast difference between "heaven" and "earth"; between "God" and "man"; between "sin" and "righteousness"; between "corruption" and "incorruption"; between "death" and "Life." All *words* to clothe my thinking, my wondering, my problems, my questions, my realizations. What, you, *you,* think of *heaven*? Surely, I may, and I will; and I will lift up my eyes and see. For there are meeting places; oh, many of them, glorious trysting places, all busy in teaching me the alphabet of heavenly things and teaching my earth born eyes to see the Divine.

It is there at the Manger that I learn the letter A, my first letter for the School of Life but the Eternal A,[1] and vision of earth beholds the opened heavens dropping down the Gift. God meets man there, reveals, teaches, translates. Destination! And every letter-lesson along the way till I come to the Hill of the Cross.

There I learn my letter S[2] at His second cradle built

[1] A—Alpha,—The Beginning; the first letter in the Greek alphabet
[2] S—Soter,—The Saviour; more symbolically the X,—The Saviour

for Him by man; and vision of earth beholds the heavens closed, frowning, black, impenetrable, but earth opened, rent and torn, to take back its creatures, sin and death. GOD meets man there, reveals, teaches, translates. Destination!

I retreat; would escape this, thinking all is vain; and go down into the Valley of the Shadow, and there at the Tomb I learn my letter N[3] at the last cradle made for Him by man; and vision of earth beholds the earth burst open to yield That which it cannot hold, Life! God meets man there, reveals, teaches, translates. Destination!

Then on,—short journey now; another Hill to surmount, and when earth-ear hears the last Farewell, heart and soul catch the strains of Heaven's Host and I learn my last letter O,[4] and earth vision beholds the open Portal—the welcome home to the disciple, faithful, and true. God meets man there! Revealing? Teaching? Translating? No longer; for "faith is lost in sight; and patient hope is crowned; and everlasting Light, His glory sheds around."

Oh, that the greeting may be to me, "Enter into the joy of thy Lord." "Who for the *joy* set before him. . . . " For the joy set before me!

---

[3] *N*—Nike,—The Victor
[4] *O*—Omega,—The Ending; the last letter in the Greek alphabet

At Bethany

✛

INSPIRATION : *The Home at Bethany.*
The Parable of the Talents,—
Matthew 25:14-30.

✛

MEDITATION

THE Journey has been resumed. We have gone forward on our way after the quiet time at the Wayside. The hard way has been ploddingly conquered step by step. The great objective,—Jerusalem? or?,—ever before and even at a distance bearing its influence, quickening expectation, or driving home the solemn sensing of impending ill. Hour after hour has passed; the day is aging; and now it is almost eventide as we enter the little village of Bethany.

Before us stands a doorway wide open, framing eager faces and outstretched welcoming arms: the last open doorway for the Traveler till they *force* Him through one and *carry* Him through another! But here the warmth of loving welcome meets, surrounds, enfolds Him. Some people were good to Him after all! The Road isn't all hard and tiring and depressing and aloneness; there are sunny hours even on this King's Highway,—even though they be few.

There stands Lazarus, "*his* friend,"—possessive his!
—and what better name today? Some one else was
once called "the friend of God!" What tender, adoring love in his steady gaze! How all-giving the hand
stretched out to draw Him in! "Oh, come to my heart,
Lord Jesus; there is room in my heart,—*home,*—for
Thee." No spoken word between these two; a bond
unique in this world unites them: what mystic seal
welds them as one; what vision of the Beyond fuses
their brotherhood; what sacrament seals their communion! One "whom *he* raised from the dead" meets
one who is yet to taste of death, but who already has
conquered, is master of it! The Brotherhood of the
Empty Tomb. My Jesus,—welcome!

And there stands Mary; patiently, quietly waiting
for His kindly glance and word, that she, too, may offer
her heart's welcome. Here, too, is a mystic, sacramental bond, a *double* drinking from the Well-spring
of Life, first at His feet, then at His hands; a ministry
that met and conquered life's severest test and was
crowned with life's completest gift; her heart has had
its passion, cross and tomb and in the fore-thrown
shadow of His own He had stopped to heal the wound
and rebind the cords and empty that tomb. The Mary
who *knows* waits to welcome Him and then hurry
in to Martha. All is excitement; and now *she* tells
busy Martha, "The Master is here." And Martha,
alive with desire to welcome Him with every comfort and refreshment that generous, fullest love can

provide, hurries forward to add her glad word of welcome.

What a trinity of friends this eventide brings the Traveler into this open-hearted home, His own if He but will.

Adoring immolation,—what would not Lazarus do for Him! What does he have that *He* has not given him and will not give to Him on the instant again?

Adoring faith,—what in the wide, wide world could ever shake that, or rob it of one instant's loyalty?

Adoring service,—what could He desire that would not instantly be done?

And is not this trinity the making of the heart-home where He abides the welcome possessor of one's giving one's all? Everything they have is gladly, unqualifiedly, unstintingly His. The best they have is none too good, but *it is* the welcome and giving of love; and the bond of union is the bond of having found and knowing, each in his or her own unique way, the all-giving, the all-sufficient Master, their,—his, her, her,—Jesus: Friend,—Lord,—Master.

The Home of the Open Door on the King's Highway,—here I would enter with Him and listen, too, at His feet this eventide; and may the door of my heart be as wide open and as welcoming, and may I learn of Him that I too may offer Him my trinity of glad giving.

The Five Talents of the Fellowship
The First Talent : Listening to the Voice

✤

INSPIRATION : *Hear, and your soul shall live.*
Speak, Lord, for thy servant heareth.

✤

MEDITATION

EVENTIDE; one more day is done. Its busy hours
are over; its cares are laid away; now the quiet
and peace and bond of love and communion. Here
in the quiet of this home,—a moment's pause on our
Journey,—the day's things are laid away with the light-
ing of the evening lamp, a gentle, kindly, flickering
flame, just a tender glowing. A circle of friends gathers around the Master, close to Him, and listens. All
is still save His voice of grace and life. He is looking
out through the open doorway,—into the dark. Echo
. . . "Watchman, what of the night?" Echo . . .
"How beautiful upon the mountains are the feet of
him that bringeth good tidings, that publisheth peace
. . ." Does Zion know? It's very dark over there
in the corner; terribly dark outside of that doorway!
Does Zion know? Will Zion listen? . . . "The peace
of God which passeth all understanding . . . !"

As the Master gazes out and on, He speaks. What

memory words He recalls for these days:—"He that heareth these sayings of mine"; . . . "The words that I speak, they are . . . life"; "He that hath ears to hear, let him hear" . . . "Ye are my friends if ye do whatsoever I have commanded you" . . .

At the Wayside, I listened to learn the way of discipleship; and now He is building the disciple-life. For each course to be laid in this structure He has a gift, a "talent." A talent? Yea, a gift from Him to me; His own still though given to me to use as my own . . . but for Him. And do I not gain benefit in the using?

What is this First Talent? I hear much of doing; but that is not, cannot be, first. Before I can do, I must learn. But neither is learning the first; for before I can learn and while I am learning I must listen. "Be still, and know that I am God." Yea, even to *know* I must listen . . . and hear "the voice of gentle stillness." "Hear, and your soul shall live." . . . In these days; all along the King's Highway.

This is the quiet time of the soul, this eventide spent at His feet. With Lazarus, and Mary and Martha and the others I am going to the never-failing Spring to drink of the water of life. But my thirst:—what sort of listener am I? There is but one way to listen *and hear*. But once He told us,—do you remember?— there were four ways to *listen*! Do you remember when He told us about the Sower sowing the Seed and how it fell? Yes, the places were there,—*the places where it fell*,—and there were four sorts, but only one where it stayed and grew and bore:—four kinds of listeners, but only one that really heard.

Now isn't that a cross-section of the day of life?—mine?—yours? O, the sounds, the noises, the voices; the calls, the cries, the invitations! How they all fall on my ear and how I discriminate and listen to what I will amid all the clamor of the day!

O the sounds of the world beyond that open doorway; of that dark; of these hours! All the sounds *He* had to listen to; the sounds I hear!

Soon the shout of the crowd,—and then the howl of the mob!

The acclaim of the disciples,—then the denying voice of Peter!

The singing of the Children of the Temple,—and then the weeping of the pitying women!

The sound that Judas heard,—and the sound that Jesus heard when Judas spoke!

The lofty strains of the Temple Choirs,—and then the hard voices of the priests.

Where are the songs of the birds and the quiet whisperings of the mountainside and fields? Here is the turmoil of the city; the inflamed mob; the mad "Crucify!"; the world din: jeer, scoff, judgment; crunch of road; scrape of dragging cross; sharp command; sighs of pity; the hammer clap; the thud; angry nature, above, below, within!—blasphemy, derision, sneer; . . . ah, at last a gentle prayer, a soft fallen tear! *His* voice,—a sigh,—and all is still! "Be still, and know that I am God."

But when will I hear "the voice of gentle stillness?" Not in the tempest of Babel; not in the convulsions of life's turmoil; but only in the quiet hour, the hour of communion, the steady, waiting, welcoming *broad field* of the open heart, the harmony of receptivity. Then the Revealer leads me beside the still waters to the green pastures of the Vision of God.

Only in quiet lowliness of spirit and in the stillness of hungering faith and in the patient waiting of love may one perceive the Infinite. Here purified of the clamor of world and time, cleansed of the noise of life's commotion and flesh's warring, may I apprehend Holiness; for it is the pure in heart only who shall see God. The realization as I receive into my soul is reality,— Immanuel! God with us!—Jesus,—"He shall save!"— Christ,—"Behold, my Servant!"—Good Shepherd,— "I am come to seek and to save!"—Teacher!—"No man spake as he!"—Lord,—"Thou hast the words of eternal life!" Lord, speak to me. "Speak, Lord; for thy servant heareth."

Discipleship,—the First Talent
  It is given to me to listen;
    to commune with Him;
    to drink the waters of life;
    to be taught the way;
    to be nourished unto life;
    to be strengthened for the day;
    to be knit to Him.

The Five Talents of the Fellowship
The Second Talent : Learning the Lessons

✠

INSPIRATION : *This is life eternal, that they should know thee. . . .*

> *I am meek and lowly in heart. . . .*
> *Be ye holy, for I am holy.*

✠

MEDITATION

THE great Objective,—during these day one thinks of that as Jerusalem and "the things that there come to pass." Well, that is most certainly true, as long as I go far enough. For no more is the Cross the great Objective than is the Garden; and no more is the Tomb than is the Temple. The great objective is the "Victory which he hath obtained for us" over Cross and Death and Tomb. "This is life eternal that they should *know* thee and Jesus Christ whom thou hast sent" . . . "Whom to know *is* everlasting life!" Every association with the Master, every event in the Traveler's way, every word the Teacher speaks, centers in this Objective; and here I become possessed of the Second Talent.

The trouble is not to translate these experiences with the Master into terms of comprehension and application and fruitage, but to gain the approach to them that guarantees comprehension and application and fruitage. This the Master commits to me, once I have found that the beginning of my communion with Him is the open, listening heart, the completely surrendered self to His possession and direction: the readiness to be possessed, then equipped, then sent forth.

In my own relation with Him, by His grace, is to be realized the humble counterpart of His pregnant relation with His Father. As Master, so disciple, is quietly divinely true here. It is of His grace and goodness that this may be so and that from smallest beginnings it is nourished tenderly, strengthened graciously, preserved victoriously to the stature of manhood in all its fullness in Himself. And it is in His school of life, the school of His life, that He holds up to me and shares with me; and it is in the school I attend in my life that now He shares with me, too, and where He teaches me the lessons of *His* school, that I learn experience and comprehension, experience and application, experience and fruitage.

First steps must be guided and assisted and encouraged and protected before first steps grow from toddling and stumbling to surer walking; but there must be will to essay the first steps and willingness to be helped and to learn the how, not willfulness to attempt it alone; else, perhaps, the defeats and failures will result in discouragement and an effort to progress some other way. But where the assistance is of gracious interest, more, of loving concern, and the encouragement takes the form of comfort and inspiration, failures become accomplished gains, grow into incentives, develop mastery; discouragements are aids to developing strength and courage; and the double process serves to teach the bond of union: a dependence on Him that is not discouraged, inspiration and aid from Him that are not denied.

So I learn to know my Teacher, and His teaching; and as I learn this, I learn something needed for myself and in myself, and for my coming: First, the humility that realizes its own weakness, insufficiency and dependence upon Him; for it is only in such humility that His lessons and the lessons from His life may be apprehended. And then, the next step, healing. Shorn, cleansed of the self-reliant and self-assertive, I go far beyond mere weakness; back of them to the source of my troubles and ills: conditions and sicknesses of soul and heart, of will and desires, of life. Sin?—yes, *sin*, in all its blighting power, its wounds and diseases, its searing and its death. To Him Who is far, far more than Teacher, Who becomes my Physician and is *my Saviour*, I come to gain and learn His healing touch. And that requires the third step, which becomes a station. This is the life relationship; this is the breath of communion; this is the heart bond of complete accord.

The Five Talents of the Fellowship
The Third Talent : Losing the Limitations of Life

✛

INSPIRATION : *I can do all things through Christ who strengtheneth me.*

✛

MEDITATION

GLORIOUS liberty!—the load lifted from the soul; the shackles of slavery removed; the penalty of guilt paid; the servitude of sin ended,—*freedom!*—the gift, the benediction, the inspiration, the possession, the grave responsibility of new-found sonship, privilege! Pilgrim, are you ready for that? Can you be trusted with that? Nevertheless that is the next-given Talent of the Fellowship, a loosing from the limitations of life.

Oh, what joy it is, what exhilaration, to throw out one's arms wide to all the world, and looking the future full in the face breathe in the air of freedom! Yes, Pilgrim; but, from what? There's where my exhilaration needs to be tempered, and lest I be so securely sure and heedlessly certain and falsely persuaded and begin to boast my freedom and the ever tempting "I,"—like "Abraham's seed," I need to realize that I am just as weak in my liberty as I was in my bonds, and just as needy of the love and ministrations of my Emancipator now as I was before He set me free. And I need to *remember* not only the past but past condition in all its ill and corruption, in all its misery and godlessness, in all its panic and terror, in its fatal finality. He who tells me that He *is* the Door also tells me of a door that is shut!

So weld thee new shackles of living remembrance, and be bought with the Price to the new servitude of glorious love, O new-found child of God!—the freedom of the "Bond-servant of Christ." Bind thee to Him with thy "I *give* myself to thee"! shackle thee to Him with the Drop of Blood that is wholly thine; harder and more enduring than steel be the bonds that rivet thy heart, thy life, to His. Oh free slave! glory in thy freedom; rejoice in Love's servitude. *Therein* is the exhilaration!—what rapt desire to possess and to move to the giving of all. The heart bounds free, to spend itself in giving. The ear opens to the Traveler's "Ephatha," to hear the harmony of new life and new world. The dumb tongue is loosed to glorify, to testify, to invite, to constrain, to pray, "O could I speak the matchless worth, O could I sound the glories forth which in my Saviour shine."

I lose every limitation when I put on me every mark of, and binding to, His service. My weakness becomes His strength; my hesitation His boldness; my poor faculties and abilities the very means to His ends. I can do all things in *that* spirit. O Pilgrim, know it: *all* things,—conquer the ever present temptation; conquer the ever trying self; conquer the ever attacking world; . . . in Him . . . for Him.

No rod in my hand, like that in Moses', to drive home in awe the limitless power and conquer all opposing,—the mighty revelation of the Divine. No; no rod in my hand. Now "simply to His Cross I cling" and in that glory. Signed with the Cross, I hold the cross; and sign with the cross ✠ my every hour, my every purpose, my self consecrated to the freedom of Love's bondage. "In that sign *conquer*"— yes; but only if it is vitalized reality that has impressed the fadeless image on my heart. Far rather,—"more than conquerors through him that loved us."

O, the boundless possibilities of the redeemed soul and life! Treasure this Talent, Pilgrim; and "occupy till I come." Even so, Lord Jesus.

The Five Talents of the Fellowship
The Fourth Talent : Lifting the Burdens From the Heart

✠

INSPIRATION : *Abound more and more . . .*
Love one another . . .
Bear ye one another's burden . . .

✠

MEDITATION

OH, NO, Pilgrim; you aren't living with your head in the clouds and walking on air; and you are far from mingling with the Hosts of Heaven and the Glorious Company of the Apostles and the Goodly Fellowship of the Prophets. Care!—you'll be startled to realize all too suddenly that you are a candidate for the Noble Army of Martyrs; and the realization of that can work *two* ways!

There are just two things, Pilgrim, that can defeat every purpose of the Traveler in you and every gift the Master makes you. The one is a pious, platitudinous, self-hypnotizing security, and the other is an impractical, over-misting optimism. Both of these blind, and blindness is worse than darkness here. So to me is given a Fourth Talent.

Pilgrim, your old master was an hard overlord,

heavy-handed, all-exacting, satanically guileful, and
gleeful at your toil and sweat; and never a word for
you when the day was over and you had done his
will. You could find your own corner,—and there
wasn't any brightness there!—and rest, if you called
that rest! Where? and with what? Your conscience?
your accomplishments? your earnings? Come to think
of it, what were your earnings after all?

But your new Master! "My yoke is easy and my
burden is light; and ye shall find rest unto your souls."
"By this shall all men know that ye are my disciples,
if ye have love one to another."

Now right here is the Fourth Talent. Loosed from
the limitations of life brings a temptation and the peril
of another fatal failure. So this Talent is one of safe-
guarding,—the intense activity of the freed one, the
new slavery, the work of love, the ministry of mercy.
His benediction descends to rest upon my burdened
heart and to lift those burdens away, be they sin-
slavery, self-slavery, or what they may. His yoke re-
places the removed load; but it is shared with me and is
no burden but privileged, communal opportunity, the
very essence of the Fellowship. The ministry to me
that stills my troubled heart, removes my fears, heals
my wounds, wipes away my tears, comforts me amid
earth's sorrows, brings the Peace that passeth understanding; and this all is seed planting unto fruit bearing. That is the *giving* of this Talent.

My words and my acts, my hands and my feet, my

heart and my life, my service, my concern are to spend themselves in the administration of this Talent. Here is the busy life that will make me face the things of the common day, that will keep my feet solidly on this old earth, and my head will go right into the clouds and storms of *my brethren's* storms and tempests. Well, let them beat about us; that's the idea, that *we* weather them *together*, that we help each other, that we all carry the yoke . . . "workers together with him!"

The Talent of Lifting the Burdens from the Heart,— what an inspiring servitude. Oh, to see the smile come out of tears! To feel the clasp of full brotherhood; To experience the joy of partnership! To know, to garner, the accomplishment of ministry in some burdened one . . . for *Him*. "So shall ye be my disciples." "Bear ye one another's burdens" . . . The Brotherhood of Heart's Burden Lifters.

The Five Talents of the Fellowship
The Fifth Talent : Life's Fullness in Love

INSPIRATION : *I am come that they might have life,
and that they might have it more
abundantly.*

*Inasmuch as ye have done it unto
one of the least of these my brethren,
ye have done it unto me.*

✝

MEDITATION

HE THAT *loveth* his life shall lose it; and he that
hateth his life in this world shall keep it unto
life eternal."

"He that *findeth* his life shall lose it; and he that
loseth his life *for my sake* shall find it."

Hard sayings? Am I dealing with paradoxes or con-
tradictions?

But here is the Fifth Talent, the final, the complet-
ing, the culminating Gift. If I go out on my way de-
liberately to find it, I will never possess it; but if I
go on His way, seeking to follow where He has trod,—
the King's Highway!—I will possess it; and none shall
ever take it from me. "Thou wilt show me the path
of life: in thy presence is fulness of joy; at thy right

hand there are pleasures for evermore." "For with thee is the fountain of life . . ." That is it! There's the "secret": "Thou"—"with thee."

Here in this blessed Bethany home where we are tarrying this little while on our journey such terms as "death" and "life" are no strangers! I look at Lazarus;—what flashes into my thought? I look at Mary; —what remembrance does that bring? I look at Martha;—and still another! Death and Life! Faith and confession at the grave! The embodiment of spending love! And then my look centers on the Traveler;—life, death, LIFE!

As HE quietly builds the fabric of our Fellowship, all the while compounding His gifts, I realize that He is building a structure of living service for me and building *in* me; rather, should I not confess, rebuilding? For with every course He lays on His sure foundation, something I have already laid is displaced, so that all that I have built passes away to give place to all that He makes of me.

So it has been all along the Highway; every step is marked with the rebuilding of men's and women's lives, and all into one tremendous Purpose, one *everlasting* Goal, a fabric which neither time nor man and all that they possess can mar or cause to decay.

As I sit at His feet, my bosom heaped full with His given Talents, and now, this last, I am concerned with my own relation to Him in the light of these gifts and of this last. Each one of them inspires a genuine response, and the response is given not of duty or compulsion but for His sake, for love's sake. Ah, there it is again! And this response is productive, and just that much more productive as I lose sight of myself,— a fruitage without will and attention? No! He gives the attention; and it is His will that the branch bring forth fruit,—that it may *remain*!

And now, here at His feet, looking down the vista of these coming days, this last Talent. What is the "secret" of life? What but finding Life; and I know what that is now. What was His secret? Have I found that, too? It is possible to be discovered!—but it dawns on one like the golden splendor of consummation will some day dawn, wholly as the gift of Him Whose own discovery is made mine own. Meantime shafts of glorious light are pointing the way: the listening, the learning, the loosing, the lifting,—all merge in the living,—living love, loving life. "The life that I now live in the flesh I live by the faith of the Son of God, who loved me, and gave himself for me." *His* daily "inasmuch" to the "whosoever" becomes, *is* my daily "inasmuch" for the "whosoever"; for the fulness of life is in the ministering of the Talents He entrusts to me.

Resuming the Journey : Olivet's Brow

✛

INSPIRATION : *He came unto his own, but his own
received him not.*

*It is required in stewards, that a
man be found faithful.*

Read: ST. MATTHEW 10.

✛

MEDITATION

ANOTHER morning has come. Our little Company
once more is on its way. The King's Highway
winds its way on, on, ever upward. Olivet must be
climbed before we can enter Jerusalem. Yes; Olivet
must be climbed before I can enter Jerusalem! Why
did I repeat that? Don't *you* see?

The crowd is growing; every doorway in Bethany
contributes some one to swell the numbers. The noise
of voices and the excitement increase as we go along.
Jerusalem! just beyond that mountain,—almost there.
If we only were! But first we must climb the hill.

The Traveler presses on; now and then a glance at
His companions, almost a question in His look; but
steadily on goes He. He, too, is seeking a City! At
last the summit, and then around that curve, and,
behold, Jerusalem! "The city of the great King!"

The crowd stops involuntarily; exclamations on every side: joy, praise, gladness; shout and song fill the air! "Whither the tribes go up . . ." At last, almost there! Journey's end for them: attainment. But what for *Him*? Journey's End? Not there; but atonement. And why, that for *Him*? And what of us? Well, that remains to be seen! Will I carry on, faithfully, or fail Him?

Quietly He has drawn aside from the road and from the crowd, and, behold, as He stands and gazes, He weeps. A profound stillness holds His little Company as we gather close around Him. His tears; His precious tears! As each one falls, the tolling of Jerusalem's knell. "O, Jerusalem, how I would have gathered thee." "O Jerusalem."—"It is required in stewards, that a man be found faithful!"—and the fate, the penalty, of unfaithfulness.

Mighty, stirring days, and hours are ahead, the sifting days and hours. From the glorious scene of the jewel-set City, His glance turns to us. Faithfulness!—? In the days and hours ahead? We, the Company, the Peters and Johns and Andrews and Judases, the you's and me's;—what of this discipleship, this fellowship, of which I've learned? Will it stand the test of crucial hours and events. *It* surely will, as He has built it! BUT will *I* stand the test of that discipleship?

Our little Company lingers here; there is no hurry; our future waits! It is sure! But the crowd hurries on; their future is the will-'o-the-wisp of the moment!

They hear the voice of desire urging them on; we hear His searching voice as He measures the value and strength of our devotion to Him: of our faith, our obedience, our love, our constancy, 'mid impending things. For His vision is all-seeing: ours sees only distant Jerusalem!—the rest is imagination!

All along He has been building the Community of His Life and Service in us. We have not failed to hear just those things we must know if we are to be His followers and companions. There have been testings all along the way, but these have been the tests that have been turned to the development of an abiding value in us. Have we yet met the tests of those things the forces of evil can marshal when driven to desperation? Have I ever had to stand alone?

There have been gifts, too. O, the promises which accompany the privileges and the encouragement energized by His unstintingly placed confidence. Has not this all been preparation for coming things? Now comes the sifting time and the use of what I have been given; now comes the test of my innermost, my most vital union with Him: of the *me* in what He has given me. What will I do if I should be separated from Him? Where am I going to be as we go into the City; walk its streets; enter its Temple; mingle with its holiday crowd? Rank after rank is marshaling to *welcome* Him,—and then assault Him! Will I be ignored? "Surely thou art one of them!" Will I be faithful?

The Five Tests of Faithfulness
The First : The Test of Confession

✠

INSPIRATION : *But whom say ye that I am?*

> *Whosoever shall confess me before men, him will I confess before my Father who is in heaven. But whosoever shall deny me before men, him will I also deny before my Father which is in heaven.*

✠

MEDITATION

IT IS brought home to me that *He* is depending on me in all things, and that my companionship is but one of these. It is brought home to me that days and hours will come, perhaps very soon, when I will be all alone, even without the support and inspiration of a fellow disciple at my side, when the meeting of the issue will be *my* privilege and responsibility, and *only mine*. It is brought home to me that there is vastly more ahead of me in my discipleship than the meditative, quiet hours of communion and rapt vision. The days are coming upon me, too, when I must carry this with me and in me into my home, my street, my town, my work, my every day, my contacts and relationships, and meet *every thing* that comes in the course of daily life as His disciple. I can't be a visionary then; I can't be a mere *follow*-er then: the disciple faces the discipline; the steward becomes the soldier; the follower becomes the standard-bearer; the dreamer becomes the testifier; the visionary becomes the missionary. It is the Test of Confession that I face. The Teacher has taught. The scholar has gone to school. How much has he learned?

Coming days and hours visualize before me as He talks to us. He pictures me down in the City with Him. All around the excited, shouting, acclaiming crowd. Some one grabs hold of my arm, "Who is that?" Oh, it is easy to make the good confession when enthusiasm is running high and all about are smiling faces and acclaim, and apparently no hostility. One can answer even the curious instantly and courteously!

He pictures me in the Temple. Religion everywhere: spiritual, professional, habitual, commercial; Sabbathized, popularized, kitchenized! The priests are ministering; the Levites are singing; the harpists are playing; the rabbis are teaching; the crowds are surging through the courts and galleries; the shekels are falling into the treasury; the grand entrance is crowded with vendors and buyers; even the back exit has its activity, the roast meat of the sacrifices is disposed of there! Reformation, cleansing, zeal! The Test of

Confession is not hard to meet when the holy fire of righteousness burns!

But somehow I become separated from Him and our Company in all this commotion. Pushed, jostled, I enter one of the gallery alcoves. Here the turmoil has not entered. Religion is being expounded: "Thus saith the Scriptures"; "Thus saith the fathers"; "Thus and so is the teaching of this school!" I hear. Is it the TRUTH? Is it the JESUS-TRUTH?—the LIVING TRUTH? the Truth that sets men free? The Test of Confession faces me! Argument?—away with that! But how will I meet it,—or fail to meet it?

I see myself seeking our Company. As I go strange men surround me,—"This is one of them!" Glory or shrinking? Fear or happy privilege?

And so I make my way back to the Trysting-Place, realizing that the disciple *is* a marked man and one other thing comes home to mark this,—the supremacy of the service, to which I have given myself. I need not only to know but to hold fast to the Faith,—to be ready to give to every one that asks me the reason for the hope that is in me. Branded in my heart must be the marks of my servitude: "Whose I am; whom I serve."

The Five Tests of Faithfulness
The Second : The Test of the Commission

✤

INSPIRATION : *Go into the village over against you*
. . . If any man say ought unto you,
ye shall say, The Lord hath need of
of them . . .
   Go into the city to . . .
   Go into the highways . . .
   Go into all the world . . .

✤

MEDITATION

IT IS well, realizing the fullness and completeness of
whose I am and whom I serve, to sit here quietly
and come to a basic understanding of myself. Accepting the Commission, and direct heritage of the
Fellowship, is going to be a far-reaching and ever-re-
maining engagement of no one or few parts of me but
of all of me, and for no brief or longer part of my
time but for all of my time. I bring my whole self to
this. Yes, that I have learned and realized and agreed
to gladly! Stop! "Gladly?" Is that the rock-bottom
of vital honesty? No retrenchment? No hesitation?
No reservation?

Very well; that's a whole-souled, happy commitment then! Then I bring my life to this. That, too, I have already learned; all of my days; wherever I am, whatever I do; in the broadest, fullest statement of life, every possible relationship which I create or which is created for me. There again,—and remember what it involves!—no retrenchment?—hesitation?—reservation? There cannot be, if I give all. And it does not "annoy" me to realize that I have transferred the title of ownership of *my* time, and that *His* time is being administered by me! Oh, the length and the breadth . . . !

Now Pilgrim, face the fact of your commission? Broad, full, complete, and yet so definitely, even minutely, detailed. Where will you go that it is not effective? What will you do that *that*, too, is not operative? Can you ever lose it for as much as a second? And just what is it? You ask that question now as if the programme of your life had to be laid out before you in explicit detail?—as if you had to be shown definitely the this and that of every day: this is here; that is coming; this is around the corner; that is coming next week? Then go back, while you have time,— HIS?—yours?—and learn all over again from the beginning! You have not caught *your* part yet.

Whether I'm sent to gather up the crumbs, or fetch the ass, or to go into the city to follow a man bearing a pitcher, or to stand before kings and declare *His* glory, or before the scoffer and maintain *His* truth and honor, that need not so much be shown me as that I need to be ready to and do accept the given privilege-commission as it appears and when it appears. In *His* plans and handling, "little things" are vitally, vastly important. In his salvaging, humble tasks, unknown acts, unheralded testimony, crumbs, drops of water, tears, one soul, one life; beggars, cast-aways, wrecks, a thief,—become the treasures of the Eternal Garner. In His divine Love, which transcends and therefore routs all human wisdom, He takes one like me and puts me in the way of gathering a crumb for Him, or wiping away a tear, or declaring His Way to some wanderer, or of going after a lost sheep for Him,—puts me in the way of *garnering a jewel for Him*! And who knows when opportunity will come or when it is not present? O, Pilgrim, do not go about looking for things to do, or for chances to do big things, or to be a hero!

"Sing, pray, and keep His way unswerving;
So do thine own part faithfully,
And trust His word; though undeserving,
Thou yet shalt find it true for thee."

That's it: the singleness of His service is your inspiration; the practice of His religion,—your religion, the religion you profess,—your daily employ.

The Five Tests of Faithfulness
The Third : The Test of Constancy

✠

INSPIRATION : *Satan hath desired to have you, that*
he may sift you as wheat . . .
Will ye, too, go away?

✠

MEDITATION

NOW comes the Test which searches the depths of
my soul's allegiance, which with relentless and
unswerving compulsion and almost malign deliberation
calls my faith, my trust, my devotion, my sacrifice,—
myself, as I claim to be in my Lord,—to the mark, and
forces me to a searching, gruelling duel for supremacy.
It *is* a fight! Here on this Hillside, overlooking that
City, its streets, its palaces and halls, the little garden,
and the hill beyond: the Mighty Stage of the Tremendous Tragedy-Victory; these Coming Days, the atmos-
phere; this very hour, the herald;—here think of this
Test! It is *fight*!—and there is going to be fighting
for you, my Pilgrim, too; whether now or later, *it*
will find you.

Sing for preparation! "Sure I must fight if I would
win; increase my courage, Lord"; but better, far better,
before a single step is taken, to remember while you

sing your courage up, the battle is not always to the strong and that here is a sufficiency that makes weakness perfect strength if it is apprehended and appropriated.

The Test of Constancy! *my* constancy!—when will it meet me? If I knew would I be ready for it? Would I rush into it with the rashness of over-confidence and enthusiasm to win for Him? Great chance to win for Him, to glorify Him! And knowing it would be hard and searching to the very depths, would I go in with zeal: the harder the better; the more searching the greater the inspiration? Seems there's something wrong somewhere here! Would it be with me? But there is not the test.

It is not coming with blare of trumpets to discover itself to me, nor to warn me of the attack; there is no old-fashioned chivalry of battle in this duel; and there is no chance of escape when it does come and no weakness of consideration on the part of the enemy! Two things are involved, "My Lord and I," His honor and my loyalty; and know right now that I am as nothing, good for nothing, and worth nothing even to the enemy, apart from my love and devotion to Him! If I do not possess these, be sure no test will ever come!

These Days, this City, our going in and out with the Traveler, mark all these well; they are the mirror of life. I am wondering whether the little Company would have run away if they had known. Would I have run away, had I been there? I'm wondering whether it would have made any difference with Judas if he had been told all about it. And Peter,—Peter of all the Company!—would it have been any different if John or some one else had whispered, "It's the Test?"—and yet, Peter had been forewarned. Even self-offered loyalty fails to meet the Test!—what of a vaunted enthusiasm for meeting it? "Sift you as wheat" . . . grains in the hands of determined enmity to be thrown about at will! Oh, pray that in the throwing about the chaff will be rid away and living grain be left!

The Test and me. To abide faithful, steady, firm, unswerving in purpose and action, in devotion and love when the issue would rob me of something precious to me to which I want to cling; when for Jesus' sake I am called to *sacrifice*, will, purpose, ambition, possession, attainment, what ever it be, to *sacrifice*! "Endure hardship as a good soldier of Jesus Christ." Ah, don't boast, "Though all forsake thee, yet will not I." Search your soul, Pilgrim; plumb it to the depths yourself; be honest with yourself. You must be that if you want to be that with *Him*! What are you going to do with Jesus? Remember what they did . . . forsook Him! Judas' way, sold Him; Peter's way, denied Him; Pilate's way, crucified Him! What are *you* going to do with Him?

Only when I have come to the completeness of self-surrender will I have the faith and patience that endure and the hope and loyalty that are steadfast.

And what of the Traveler these Days? Behold, He is teaching and showing me!—giving me an example that I should follow His steps.

The Five Tests of Faithfulness
The Fourth : The Test of Self-Emptying, Self-Conquering Humility

✤

INSPIRATION : *I have given you an example, that ye should do as I have done to you.*

The servant is not greater than his Lord . . .

But he that is greatest among you shall be your servant.

Read—ST. MARK 10:35-45.

✤

MEDITATION

FOUR places:—Where we are now, here on the Mountain Side;—prevision brings the other three, where we soon will go: The Upper Room and the Feet Washing; the Garden and "Not my will but thine be done"; the Cross and silence that holds me fast bound as I think of Him and His giving . . . "unto death, even the death of the Cross."

Now wells the echo,—echo!—echo!—through all the days along all those paths, *now* to be translated, glorified: "Blessed are the meek, for they shall inherit the earth." Assertion or pregnant prophecy? "HE" shall inherit the earth!—that meek and lowly One;—

[100]

the conquest of the All-giving One: "Thou are worthy to receive. . . ." ". . . to take up thy power and reign."

What place has Pilgrim here?—to sit and listen? to accompany and behold? These Days and Events concern me and my Companions; but our experiences are those of the "Company"; our tests are merest child's play compared with the Traveler's. But here, too, lest I forget and lose myself completely, there is constant calling to remembrance and constant prophetic reminder! Some day, after I have come out of the gloom of the Tragedy and the shadow of the Garden and am going forward in the glory of the Tomb, the splendor of Victory, the zeal of Achievement, some day will come my testing and passion and tragedy, too! Oh, the tragedy of forgetting!—the tragedy of self only!—the tragedy of heedless self-reliance!—the tragedy of pride rampant or offended!

How can I tell when it will come or what form it will take? All I can know is that once I begin to fall away from the sure and certain safety of complete companionship,—though He be removed, though He be out of sight, still real and sure and certain if I do my part to keep it so!—then will the field be prepared and the weakened citadel of my heart be without its guard.

Perhaps I may suddenly waken to see my brother's preferment, and wonder how that can possibly be when I have been so active and so "zealous." Why should the reward be his and not mine? Or, perhaps I may feel that I am not considered with the degree of importance that I think I should have. Perhaps . . . oh, *pride!*—prideful heart then you no longer are Pilgrim or pilgriming.

Do you want to surrender *His* Victory . . . your Victory? Do you want to undo what He has done? Do you want to assert yourself? Do you want to go *His* Way your way? Then it will be high time to hasten back into these Hours! The Test is upon you!

James and John will come again. Well, let them come; let them have place and preferment *if it be His purpose.* Smile and rejoice with them if it is to be so! But be of a rejoicing heart that you have a place *some* place *with Him*, be it where it may or what it is!

Then will come the misunderstanding, and the turning and twisting of His teachings and promises, and the scoffing and the jeering. Then will you see *Him* again, patient, humble, bearing, keeping, holding His place, owning it through it all . . . "even unto death." What of you then, Pilgrim?—your patience; your humility; your holding fast?

Then will come the aloneness. Where was a friend? "Forsaken . . . me!" Forsaken?

The Test that searches the depths, see how it was met! Self-emptying but self-conquering Humility. Only he who thus meets it will pass through and can say, "It is finished."

The Five Tests of Faithfulness
The Fifth : The Test of the Hard to Understand

✛

INSPIRATION : *What I do thou knowest not now;
but thou shalt know hereafter.*
Read—PHILIPPIANS 1:22-30.

✛

MEDITATION

ARE we ready to go on into the City? Are we ready
to tread the King's Highway once more with
Him? We have been resting, listening, and pray God,
learning. Have we been made ready? One thing
more! A last warning:—Don't carry a question mark
with you; carry something else! AND be sure, if you
pick up a palm branch, *when something happens,* that
you don't find your hands are empty! Did any one
go to the Tomb with a palm branch in his hand? Can
you carry one till then? I wonder! Perhaps that's
why one *is given* when one gets there . . . when one
gets there! When one has come through the Tests
. . . and this last.

But don't carry a question mark! Is it possible to
evade that? More numerous than the stones of the
streets, what self-asserting things they are! What

tremendous things some of them are! What staggering things! There is one answer only to them all.

But here of all places is the place for the caution,
for the whys and the wherefores will arise with almost
every step as I tread the way, from the withered Fig
Tree on, on, to the Nails and the Cross and the Tomb!

How can such things be? And when it all is over,
Why? Why was it so? How can this affect what is
asserted? Why? why, why? the ever present human
Why storming the Divine Plan and Purpose; the finite
mind staggering at the revelation of the infinite and
seeking its natural refuge; the sin-palsied heart unable to beat with the sin-conquering heart, unable to
comprehend His glorious Word; the knowledge of this
world failing before the teaching of the Eternal Wisdom. Why? Why? Why? I wonder whether God
ever stopped to ask Why? The Traveler did more than
once—but not the sort I ask!

There's a vast difference between the Why that hon-
estly seeks to know and the Why that springs from
doubt and hesitation or is the mere seeking of a passing whim or query. Yes, something else is needed for
this High Way; badly, hourly needed. And I will not
only need it as I make this holy Journey these coming
days, but I will need it all along my life's way.

And what is this?—what is the answer to every Why
I bring? "Only believe."

Wherever I am, whether in the midst of these Holy
Hours or in the midst of hours He gives me the oppor-

tunity of making holy, I must realize that the "scene" is life and the "action" is a fusion of the Divine and human. Lose sight of that and all is but a story to be analyzed as best I can with the limited, human equipment I possess,—intellect, reason, philosophy, imagination,—whatever it is,—and so meet and answer the problem to whatever degree of satisfaction or non-satisfaction I can reach. But holding fast to that, all is bathed in a new glory and possesses transcendent value. The Divine enters the *living* of the human to redeem, to restore, to regain. The Divine is constantly touching the human, and the touch is healing and peace. But the process is *Divine* and the human must learn and accept. Here is where the Way is not always open, nor is it always shown; and while one follows by faith and not by sight,—and one is the human seeking to follow the Divine, the limited following the Limitless,—the human carries its question, its hungering question. It is faith and love longing to pierce through the hard and the holy. It is humility hoping for a ray of light in the dark. It is trust clinging notwithstanding. This is not excuse-making for a natural weakness, or an evasion of the "Only believe," all-comprehending and all-demanding though it be. But the Things Hard to Understand are so beyond the ken of the commonplace of life, that even while I believe, I cry, "Lord, help thou mine unbelief," and look up . . . and the look is not without its question! Justification? Oh, no! Recognition of that which is still to be overcome in me and that which must be nurtured to overcome the other.

And there are the Whys which grow out of the rocks of disappointment, disheartenment, disillusionment! Where can I hide them? Ah, that I would hide them is proof of the guilt of those Whys. Guilt? For I know better than to give over to the victory of things that will throw me into the abyss of despair, when but one thing will lift and hold me to the Rock of Ages.

Yes, the Traveler asked Why; more than once; and again when men say he had reached the End of his Journey, he asked WHY? And now do I dare ask Why? Ah, no; not amid that desolation; not *there*! His Why! and there must have been an answer to Him; for He triumphed!

Beside Calvary and His Cross, my cross and my hills and vales are infinitesimal; but may I when I cross my hands or enter my shadows carry the heart that with the asking finds the answer in "Fear not, only believe." Amen and Amen.

The Gift : Annunciation

✣

INSPIRATION : . . . *GOD is in the midst of her* . . .

✣

MEDITATION

THE quiet of the night at Bethany is broken by the early morning call, "Arise," and soon the Traveler and our little Company are on the way once more to the Holy City. The gentle, nourishing, promising glow of the day-spring falls upon us as we top Olivet and go down and on into the valley. We cannot forget "yesterday," and as we journey on, the contrast between the Entrance yesterday and today is borne in upon us. It is tremendous . . . the difference!

What a day, yesterday! All those Hosannahs,— didn't they mean anything?—and the acclaim, even on into the very Temple courts. But what a day, today!— even with the sun's coming forth, it seems drab and heavy; there's foreboding of the impending and there's dread. And then there's that fig tree, barren, disappointing, and judged! Anything prophetic there?—as to fruitage, or disappointment, or judgment? What if *He* were to come to me expecting fruit for His *refreshment*—friendship, loyalty, service . . . and find me barren?

One thing meets us everywhere,—curiosity, craning of necks, pointing of fingers, whispering, and an excitement that runs ahead unseen but produces a meeting at every turn. But no welcoming shouts of Hosannah this morning as our little Company, led by the Traveler, climbs the Temple Way and enters the beautiful portal. The cries that greet are the shouts of the hawkers and the noise and confusion of buying and selling:—Religion yielded to the inroads of the greed of men, degenerated to the barter of worldly things for holiness, business and the holiday crowds. The world's noise drowns out the praises of Jehovah; raucous shouts still the sweet singers of Israel; and the stench of a market-place smothers the incense of the sacrifices.

Our quiet, gentle Traveler is transformed to a Man of Fire! The noise rises to a bedlam of confusion as He drives forth the traffickers and empties the Court of its desecrating mob.

Clear rings His Voice . . . "My House shall be called a House of Prayer . . . but ye have made it a den of thieves." Clear rings His Voice,—of holiness, and life, and peace. Clear rings His call to remembrance. Where is the Hosannah?

The priests gather in groups to whisper and point and plot. The parties consult to confound and condemn. The forces marshal their array. But behold the Traveler . . . "God so loved the world that he gave his only begotten Son". . . wide-spread the arms

in that cleansed Temple Court; tender and gentle that
Voice now, the Voice of the Father of the Ages to His
People . . . "I am come that ye might have life."
What a Figure He makes, there alone in the midst of
that beauty of holiness, fringed about the astonished
and confounded crowd, the splendor of the ceremoni-
ally garbed priesthood and servers, the vivid color of
class and position, the proud dress of exclusiveness and
arrogance, the glory of power and precedent, pag-
eantry and holiday display, intrenched authority and
tradition, jealously guarded privilege and place.
That . . . and HE in the midst . . . alone! "I am
come!" . . . "Daughter of Zion, behold thy salvation
cometh" . . "He is meek, and having salvation."
The Day had come when He stood forth to announce
to His People fulfilment of age-old promise long
awaited in Himself, "I am he!"

What temerity, but what giving, devotion, consecration! The zeal of God's House had eaten Him up,
but that was but one step taken in the fulfilment of the
Father's will. To this His People, "his own," in the
midst of this His House, here in all the world the one
place where His Name is enshrined and invoked by
one for His People, *He* the Giver offers them the Gift
of gifts, Himself, and bids them, Come! Annunciation! Where is the Hosannah?

The First Wound : Indifference

✦

MEDITATION

ONCE more the evening and the return to Bethany. Quiet and peace after this crowded, eventful day and after the tension and felt but unseen hand of evil and enmity everywhere. Here in the quiet I'm thinking things over. I've been one of the many about Him today; I've seen a great deal and heard a great deal; but I wonder how much I have been HIS today.

Much has been hard to understand; much I cannot fathom; but the outstanding disappointment has been to see the reaction from the storm of enthusiastic welcome of yesterday.

The Traveler has been busy, oh, feverishly busy every moment. He has not spared himself; He has been spending and giving all day long. He has been working as one in great haste! The Will of the Father, the Gift of the Father, His Call, the Way, the Truth, the Life, HIMSELF, this has been His annunciation to His People in the City of the Lord of Hosts, the City of the Great King.

But there has been a complete revulsion of feeling toward Him. Gone is all the joy of yesterday. Emotion has spent itself all so soon; the crowd's enthusiasm was but a fickle gesture; the acclaim a mere fanning of a holiday mood; the tide is at the full ebb; for everywhere today He met . . . indifference. Oh, yes, they listened, and even some asked questions; some tried to argue; and crowds followed everywhere He went. But it was a listening without response and an argument of prejudiced purpose: the holiday crowd was in no mood for such teaching as His. And the following about was born of curiosity and animosity.

What a blow this all must have been to Him! I cannot help but think of Him; for He had His hopes and expectations, and ideals and longings too. Perhaps yesterday raised momentary expectations; but He knew these people out of past experience as well as history; but who knows, perhaps there was a lingering hope . . . even though He knew the End. But expectation merged into bitter disappointment, and the dull indifference to Him and His message must have brought a still more bitter disillusionment. Was not this all a part of His desolation, too? What a People! They were hungry for the sensational, the miracle, the loaves and fishes; but for the quiet calling of the Traveler and His Life-Way, they had not come to Jerusalem for that—this was *holiday* not holy-day.

The ancient prophet, whose experiences in this very place with the forefathers of this very People had not been dissimilar to His, had named Him the Servant of Jehovah, but also the Suffering Servant; and he had previsioned this wound's infliction "in the house of his friends" . . . "When we shall see him, there is no beauty that we should desire him" . . . "we esteemed him not."

Yes, these Days, as I think of all He has been giving, and is giving to men, I must think, too, of all that has been given to Him in return! His People's gift to Him today has been an hard one to accept; it is a bitter wound in the house of His friends . . . indifference. The Hand held out, filled with bounty of Love Divine, is pierced with man's unconcern! "Is it nothing to you, all ye that pass by?"

The Gift : Presentation

✤

INSPIRATION : *And in the daytime he was teaching in the temple . . . But the chief priest and the scribes and the chief of the people sought to destroy him.*

Where your treasure is, there will your heart be also.

✤

MEDITATION

ANOTHER day has brought us back into the very center of things, the Temple. We sat a while by the roadside on Olivet's Brow last evening; and the Traveler, deeply moved by the strange harvest He had gathered during the day, talked to our listening ears but still poorly understanding hearts of hidden dangers on our paths. Troubled He is; more deeply than we have ever seen Him. He is with us but He seems far away; and yet He is always thinking of us, and feeling for us, and is keenly concerned about, *and in,* our future. What will that bring forth for Him?—for us in Him?

So, too, some of that foreboding grips us, and our little Company is tensely quiet and a bit high strung: there isn't the usual mixing and talking and free fellowship. Much like our Companion, we sit and think, or walk along quietly, still wondering.

Soon after we had passed that fig tree, now a truly barren sight;—its sought fate self-invited had come upon it;—we were sent on to Bethany alone. The Traveler remained behind, alone in the still and darkness. We knew well what He did and sought at such times, and our hearts followed and stayed with Him. These days and hours carried Him into the "closet of the closed door" even oftener than in the days gone by:—His example and the "closet" gifts of privilege and communion to us of the latter days.

Early morning found us returning again to the City, pausing now and then along the way for a word of caution or encouragement. We'll never forget these stations along the Road He Trod.

This day, too, has been crowded full. The people, crowds of them thronged about the Traveler, and watched and listened, but did not seem to know quite what to do, whether to acclaim or to deride, and so they balanced, in silence. The priests, too, some of the highest in the hierarchy, thrust through the crowd and haughtily demanded the Traveler's "credentials" and proof of His claims. The scribes and the haughty Pharisees and the condescending Sadducees followed; it looked almost prearranged; for one group after the other had some question or test or argument. There was no friendliness in their coming, nor any receptive attitude; no desire to learn born of real interest, merely the superior attitude of demanding authority and condescending superiority. While all these stood revealed as what they were in the perfect Light to Whose brightness they could not lift their eyes, others bathed in that Light. There were the children who smiled on Him; the sad whose faces reflected His given peace; the beggars who knew His goodness; the longing hearts who clung to His words. Yes, there were some few in all this mass of humankind whose interest in Him was warm and real and responsive.

But what of Him? Wherever, whenever, whoever,—one, all—the Traveler *answered*. He was zealous in ministering and teaching; now quiet in declaration; now positive in statement and claim; now sharp in rebuke; now stern in condemnation; now awful in prophetic warning, declaration and promise. He taught the Truth; He made plain the Way; He declared the Life; and then evening came. The priest and parties had left Him and the people went about their holiday plans. The Traveler and our little Company went out of the City alone.

The Second Wound : Rejection

+

MEDITATION

THE ancient prophet, previsioning the future as a reality before his very eyes, had said of Him: "He is despised and rejected of men." We have seen that today.

The Traveler has not been unaccustomed to this. All along His way His great heart has been wounded again and again by the rejection of men: rejection of His teachings, of His call, of His welcome and willing aid . . . of Himself, His claim. Men would come, linger a while, then go; few there were that stayed; few, indeed, that little Company of Jesus; and I remember how He even asked them one day whether they, too, were going away!

This attitude toward Him or rather treatment of Him seems to have been progressive, judging from His own expressions regarding the evidences along the way. First of all it seems to have had something to do with the matter of values. The Traveler's parable of the Great Supper shows that in the "excuse makers", rejecters of His invitation and giving because other things were of more concern; and this, true of the parable's personalities, was typic of the almost constant treatment by His people. And had this not been so for centuries?

Then the next evidence seems to have carried along a bit farther: evidently values had been recognized to a degree and some sort of response had been made, but the test of constancy or the continuance of that on to productiveness did not materialize. Again there was rejection. The Traveler's picture of the Sower and His Seed was not only prophetic of final attitudes but expressive of actualities. "Some fell among thorns"— as truly a description of rejection as the "excuse givers".

How often, like this day, men have come to Him with the sham-covering of supposed interest to inquire, to present a problem, to demand a test. Here in Jerusalem in these tense hours, one group after another comes before Him, as if forced to by some mighty, unseen Power, and departs . . . and departs! The Answer was given, but neither answer nor the One Who made it was acceptable. The "official" coming of Church and State and Nation. Their turning away was rejection of Him and all He is and offers and all He claims. It remained only for the people who had been championing Him more or less to add the final act to complete it. Played upon by the cunning of determined enmity, swayed by agitation and carefully laid plans, the warmth of the champions was cooled to indifference, then bought by offered sops, and at the right moment fanned to open opposition. Rejected of men . . . rejected by His own. It is indescribable—and to realize the turning away, the refusal, the casting back and the *turned* back, and to see Him still going forward on the Road He Trod notwithstanding, but so alone . . . The Rejected One!

The Hand held out, so full of giving . . . full and running over; so welcoming . . . never had it pointed the other way; so gracious . . . what blessed touches it had imparted . . . that Hand is spurned, pierced by the blow of refusal, rejection.

The Gift : Manifestation

✛

INSPIRATION : *These things have I spoken unto you, being yet present with you.*

I have manifested thy name unto the men whom thou gavest me out of the world. I have glorified thee on the earth. I have finished the work which thou gavest me to do.

✛

MEDITATION

THE Traveler knew: full well He knew all impending. As one to whom every hour is precious because He knows the remaining hours are few, He has burnt the hours of this day into heart's memories with the manifestation of Himself to us. In the quiet hours at Bethany, in the quiet hours along the road, in the quiet hours in the Garden where He loved to go,—all given to us today,—He has been shepherding us with a love that we have felt as never before. Perhaps we have begun to understand a little better.

The great city, its noises and alarms, its bustle and business, its holiday crowds, even the Temple, were far away, forgotten. This has been our last day *alone* with Him; but we did not know it. He in His love made it all our own; kept us as far away from the world as He could. Yes, He shepherded us, as we had never known it before. After a while we knew why, but today we did not; nor did we realize; nor did we listen and gather and hold as we would have, had we known!

All along the Way, He had taught; He had pictured so that we could grasp His teaching; He had actualized it in living touches and in living example; He had revealed Himself and His purpose; that which He carried so gloriously in His heart ever closely held to Himself, this, too, He had shown us; and then here, there, a flash of unearthly light had shone upon us and before us the Traveler was revealed in a majesty and splendor before which we had to bow. As men understood, so did we; but we were but earth men, we did not reach the heights.

Today manifestation has come to us in the quiet way of the heart. He has been opening our hearts and has been trying to clear away the mist from our eyes; He has been filling our ears; He has been building the Road for the future. If we had only known; if we had only sensed more than a premonition; if that quietness had been pierced, which brooded over us, hung over us almost like a suffocating pall at times, which made us restless, then worry, and we did not know why we worried; if that fear that crept in whenever His Voice stilled for a while or which seemed to grip us when He was absent from us those little times,

—if this had only been understood, what a difference it would have made in us! The age-old story of Might-Have-Been!

But here amid His friends,—such as we were,—He carried us along His Way, trying to make us see, to feel, to understand, to respond, to chord with Him! But we were very much like the people of the City and of the Temple Courts, save that we were not in-different to Him and that we did love Him. His patience with us was as longsuffering as His deep and felt love was evidenced by His desire for us to see. He was showing us the Way through sorrow and suffering and the joy of bearing and enduring; He was revealing life as conquest through the hard path of victory in weakness and loss; He was trying to make our hearts understand *His* Way: were we not journey-ing it with Him? So we were to continue! Yes, but He was our leader, our protector, our provider. Now He showed loss and separation, and we knew it would all be true! Now He sought to have us see His Way in Himself and His direction and teaching as possible for us even if He were no longer here!

There were no unearthly flashes of glory, but the perfection and beauty of His manhood, of His devo-tion, of His love, of His desire to have Himself en-shrined in us, in our hearts and life, these were here. And though we knew it not then, He was committing to us and showing us all the while, His treasures, that we might be their possessors in Him and for Him. This last day alone with Him must ever be remembered as he revealed Himself to us, and ourselves remembered as unseeing, unknowing, uncomprehending; but we listened, and He knew we loved Him the best we knew how for all our weakness then.

So today brought the little Company another gift of His giving, of His love, of His tender thought. Yes, He loved His own unto the end, ever thinking of them, ever longing to enrich them, equip, found them in His Way; and to the End He showed Himself, teaching, tending, looking forward! But we could not see; no, not as we should, our eyes were still self- and earth-holden.

The Third Wound : Betrayal

✦

MEDITATION

THEN the eventide came: the evening ever to be remembered for the gifts which were given to Him.

First came the love and welcome and ever glad readiness to minister to the traveler of Simon the Leper. Always to be remembered,—"Simon the Leper"; now healed and owned!—but still "Simon the Leper"! What a rejoicing in that name, but what a loyal heart and sound, sure refuge in him who carried it with thanksgiving and praise. Would his home be open to the Traveler? Would there be welcome there? Ah, what would he not give to HIM!—yea, before He might even ask, for that love was finding the Way.

So the Traveler and our little Company rested in Simon the Leper's house that night. Supper-time brought not only refreshment to body, but food for the spirit. Quietly the hours are passing, when the second gift is brought to the Traveler; for at His feet there rests the Woman with the Ointment. Precious is her gift, as precious as sacrifice born of discerning and realizing love can make it,—her all for Him, to honor, to cherish, and to express her own thankfulness.

Tears fell, too; but His love warmed them away, and His tender look blessed her as he received the gift of her anointing. So far, two gifts, born of love's answer to Love; two gifts of love's spending bought by Love's enrichment; two gifts to bless Him Who had translated Heaven's benediction into the reality of human experience. These two of the little Company were responding to the heart's longing of the Traveler; these two were finding the place of the Understanding Heart, and so satisfied to bring their all unstintingly, unselfishly, consecratedly to Him.

But all of the Company were not so. There were those even then who did not understand; there were those even then who had the narrow close-sighted vision of the now and were all too ready to see away and not eye to eye with Him; there were those even then who hearing Him speak would not accede to Him, would not be directed by Him, would not agree with Him; and there was one who in his heart had turned against Him.

Out into the night he had gone to prepare his gift for Him. It had been slow in coming, but it had been sure. Here, there, but all along the Way, one thing after another had slowly grown into what was now to become his final gift to the Traveler. To the gentleness along the Way, he had not warmed; nor to the love the Traveler had expended on the countless needing hearts; to His teachings he had listened, then brooded over them, then opposed and in his heart rebelled against them; to the Traveler's quiet seeking and longing for him he had slowly but surely hardened his heart. His ambitions were otherwise; his ideals were not like the Traveler's. No, the Traveler had failed *him*! Ah, how?

So out into the night to make ready the Tryst in the Garden where he would give the Traveler his gift, bought and paid for by the hand of craft and hate, sold by the hand that had grasped and had been uplifted against. Out in the dark, while the Woman was anointing and kissing His feet, while Simon the Leper was watching in tender solicitude, *he* was wrapping up his kiss in the silver of sold, eternally surrendered desire, fondling it in its precious cover, gloating over it with the hunger of satisfied hate!

One of the little Company!—and the wound he was giving Him!

The Gift : Invitation—Participation

✤

INSPIRATION : *I have given you an example, that ye should do as I have done to you.*

Take, eat, this is my body, which is given for you; this do in remembrance of me. Drink ye all of it, this cup is the new testament in my blood, which is shed for you and for many for the remission of sins; this do, as oft as ye drink it, in remembrance of me.

✤

MEDITATION

THE Upper Room has been a holy place today. The hours passed all too quickly for both the Traveler and the little Company. He poured out His heart into ours, but ours were not ready for all of His in-pouring. Deep and rich in glorious promise is the teaching He imparted, and we sat listening and watching, but we felt more the dread hanging over us than the power of His words!

All He taught was pregnant with promise of our continued union with Him. Even though He would be taken away from us or go away from us, still we

would be united with Him in a union never to be dis-
solved. To this He heartened us, but for this He also
prepared us. Here in this Upper Room He told us, too,
how we would have each other in Him, and how our
hearts set in Him were to pour out on others the
gracious love and gentleness, the glad service and concern, the bond of fellowship as He had and was and
ever would continue to pour His all for and upon us.

Shall we ever forget His humble, menial service,
when He washed the feet of the little Company? Here
was the example that should reach the heart; here was
His quiet act of invitation to imitate His willing spending; here was the benediction and glorification which
He placed upon the humblest and meanest thing done
out of love and care for another. A precious gift indeed, this His invitation to participation in His kind
of service, a participation in the life of others by the
ministry of love. So we were to live Him; so we were
to live in Him; life was to continue and be real; but
life was to be His way in us.

Then he added His tenderest grace and His most
glorious assurance. The foreboding was real; separation was impending, sure; some great and terrible
calamity was near at hand; death seemed to be stalk-
ing in the shadows,—He was going away! Yes, the
Traveler was taking the Road! . . . and we? We were
to linger and wait and live and smile and work! So
down into our very souls He reached with the Divine
Gift of His Abiding Presence. He turned our last

ritual meal into our eternal Sacramental Feast, into the Undying Invitation to the Living Participation:— Broken bread to one and all, "Take, eat, this is my body"! The cup of praise and peace to one and all,— O, mystery yet to be revealed by the coming Cross!— "The blood of the new testament shed for your sins." This as often as we would eat and drink thereof, in His memory; this the Abiding Presence and Union; this the Assurance and Fulfilment; this the Glory of His Reality, with us ever, strengthening, comforting, keeping; one in Him, He in us; all one in this our Privilege Divine! As He goes toward the Road, this is the Gift of the Going One's Abiding.

The Fourth : Disloyalty—Denial

✢

MEDITATION

BUT crowding fast upon this holy moment came the Garden and the crushing rush of terror and fear, of foreboding realized, of calamity on calamity. Our little Company, torn out of the deadened sleep of the shadowy Garden, wakes to the panic of tramping feet, welling mutter of noise of crowd, clank of steel, flash of torch. But quiet and fearless, the Traveler faces forward: had He not turned to the Road in the Upper Room?

His eye beholds, and His heart is unafraid; while our eyes drop and our hearts quake with dreadful terror. Out of that mob comes one whom we all know. What sickly smile upon that face!—it was meant for greeting! Then that kiss!—it was meant to hide that smile! As the crowd surges forward around the Traveler, arms uplifted, bonds thrown about Him, our little Company yields to the panic and flees. What a retreat! What an abject, crushing gift to give Him in the moment of His need!—and so soon after the Upper Room! *He* takes the Road alone, as He had done many a time before; but now, surrounded by crushing, crowding, hating evil, he walks the Road He had seen ahead but had never trodden before. And

His only companionship is the hatred and treachery and determined purpose of His enemies; and the parting gift of His "friends",—the little Company,—alone, forsaken, friendless!

Another hour. The Traveler stands alone before His judges. The light of the palace shines out into the dark and discovers a furtive form, slowly, indecisively coming out of the dark of that night. . . . Peter who had run away, coming back. He *had* to come back: he couldn't help it. But O, what a turn he gave to his gift to the Traveler. Starting to make it bright and glorious, slowly gaining the courage to come through as he had said he would, he suddenly covered it, then withdrew it, then gave Him something else. "I know him not!"

Thus did the Company of the Upper Room treat the Invitation, the Participation, and throw it into the dark of the lower room of self, of denial, of disloyalty, of the turned back!

The Gift : Immolation

✠

INSPIRATION : *The Hour is come that the Son of Man should be glorified.*

✠

MEDITATION

ONE of the Company wrote, after a while:—"For even hereunto were ye called: because Christ also suffered for us, leaving us an example that ye should follow his steps; who did no sin, neither was guile found in his mouth: who, when he was reviled, reviled not again; when he suffered, he threatened not; but committed himself to him that judgeth righteously: who his own self bare our sins in his own body on the tree, that we, being dead to sins, should live unto righteousness: by whose stripes ye were healed."

The Final Wound

✣

MEDITATION

AND another wrote: "For it is impossible for those who were once enlightened, and have tasted of the heavenly gift, and were made partakers of the Holy Ghost, and have tasted the good word of God, and the powers of the world to come, if they shall fall away, to renew them again unto repentance; seeing they crucify to themselves the Son of God afresh, and put him to an open shame."

The Seven Gifts of the Risen Life
The First : The Peace

✠

INSPIRATION : *Read*—ST. JOHN 20:19ff.; ST. JOHN 14:25-29.

✠

MEDITATION

THE *first* word of the victorious Christ to His own little Company of the Road He Trod—"Peace!"

But now hidden away in the Upper Room; there the doors were shut; in their hearts a complex of questions, emotions; brooding over all, fear. Suddenly the Victor is there, and a new Voice mingles with theirs—Peace!

It is the Voice out of the grave! It is the Voice that death could not still! It is the Voice of Life! It is the Voice of *Eternal* Life!—"For He hath triumphed gloriously"—and what a glorious Gift it is to their ears, to their burdened hearts.

He had prepared the little Company for these days, for this crisis in their lives, just a few evenings before; and like a benediction over troubled hearts He had soothed, "Peace I leave with you. My peace I give unto you; not as the world giveth, give I unto you." But how little they had understood. No, not as the

[133]

world giveth; *this* is the Peace of *another* world. This
is a Gift of the Risen Life,—this New Peace.

This world hears the "Peace, be still" of another
world, and the tempest must be calm! This world
must hear the "Fear not!—Peace!" and the heart must
look up. Into the lives of men, *through the closed
doors:*—sins, fears, doubts, sorrows,—enters this
Easter Gift, "Peace through the Blood of the Cross";
and a quiet is born to grow,—forgiveness of sins; allay-
ing of fears; ending of doubts; binding up of broken
hearts. "The Peace of GOD which passeth all understanding" is keeping the heart!

How glorious that voice that has been echoing down
through the centuries, "And his name shall be called
. . . The Prince of Peace . . ." Wars, tumults, were
round about, but could he have been thinking of the
mighty war of sin—merging into the War of the
Cross? And centuries before even that voice spake,
another prophet had stood in the cleft in the rock, and,
after the tumults of nature, the tempest, the earth-
quake, the fire, "the still small Voice" came to him.
That One of the Voice could control all; all obeyed
His will,—yet He came "the still small Voice"!

All, He, the Victorious Christ, holds by right of conquest . . . "He is Lord of all". . . but down through
the years comes not the stirring blasts of Victor's
trumpets, nor the thunderous tread of heavenly legions,
nor the overawing by Omnipotence, but the gentle
tenderness of the First Easter Day Greeting, "the still
small Voice"—"Peace be unto *you*"!

The Second : The Confidence

✤

MEDITATION : *Read*—St. John 15:15-19; St. Mark 16:20.

✤

SALUTATION

AS MY Father hath sent me, even so send I you. As the Father loved Him,—and loved the world;—as He trusted Him to carry His love to the world; as He knew He would do His will and the work He had given Him to do; as He sent Him to bring back His erring world,—"even so". . . "even so send I *you*"! Oh, how humble my heart is when I repeat His wondrous words.

What a Company this had been! What a Company it still was! Here had been no brave show of trust and confidence and faith in Him . . . Hidden away for fear . . . for *fear*!—the same possession that had inspired their forsaking Him and fleeing only the other night, and one had denied that he even knew Him, and only one had been at His Cross—only one, blessed, loving John.

The Great Morning had brought the excited Women and their astounding reports; but these had been to them as idle tales. And the Two, who had journeyed that Great Day at eventide had had their doubts, even

[135]

when their company became Three; ah, but not after it had become ONE!

And Thomas?

But, O, that all-forgiving, ennobling bestowal of the Victor's trust. What a benediction this revelation of His confidence in them! "Peace"—He showed them His pierced side and hands, wide open, stretched out to them—to them, pardon, restoration! "I know whom I have chosen." The fruits of His Victory now for their hands to carry; their bodies to carry His "marks"; their tongues to carry His glad tidings; their souls to carry His trust ever inspired by their Lord's commissioning.

"Even so send I you." *Me?* "Easter" has come again. Is it "Easter" in my heart? Does He ask me to carry on the work He has begun? Does He entrust, *trust,* it to me? How about the stewardship I learned about some time ago? "Even so send I *you.*"

The Third : The Presence

✠

MEDITATION : *Read*—St. John 16:5-15.

✠

SALUTATION

RECEIVE ye the Holy Ghost.
"He *breathed* on them." Proof of real life? One from the grave breathing just as they? But now, Divine Breath! Sacramental! The Breath of Victorious Life to mingle with the breath of groping men!—to brood over them; to *inspire* them; to be breathed in by them!

"Receive ye," saith He!

And now that Promise is being fulfilled;—remember, of the few nights ago? How *these* words recall *those*; but how they startle!

The Master is here,—ah, the gladness; but this Promise of His being fulfilled means He is going away . . . again. But, too, He had promised, "I will not leave you comfortless," and "he breathed on them" the Breath of Him "that is alive for ever more."

The moment's joy in having Him again, the moment's fear of losing Him again, pale before the full glory of the dawning on their souls of what this Sacramental Gift of the Risen Life means.

Are they not being commissioned? Is not *The Sent*

sending them? Are they not being consecrated by His trust? New life for them, too,—the "Easter" Life. Stirring days are ahead; out into the world; no more closed doors; no more fears; no more doubts; no more betraying Judases, or denying Peters, or doubting Thomases in this little Company. Now forward on the Way, carrying the Truth, filled with the Life!

The Fourth : The Ministry of Comfort

✣

MEDITATION : *Read*—ACTS 9:10-18.

✣

SALUTATION

WHOSE soever sins ye forgive, they are forgiven unto them.

Let my heart dwell on but one thing here. The Great Physician is prescribing for the ills of my soul. Ah, how well He knows its sicknesses, and with what sure, loving care He provides the infallible cure! "Though your sins be as scarlet, they shall be white as snow." "Son, be of good cheer; thy sins are forgiven thee." Promise and application! Now, realization.

He has borne our griefs and sorrows; He has been wounded and buffeted; He has carried the iniquity of us all; He has passed *through* the valley of the shadow of death. Why? For us—for me . . . "with his stripes we are healed."

How lovingly He applied His healing balm, His loving comfort, His mighty peace, to wounded and sin-sick hearts. Oh, all along the Road He Trod, what living monuments remain to lift up their voices in thanksgiving and praise. How the publicans and sinners thronged to hear Him. Why? Surely there was a living reason! "Neither do I condemn thee. Go, and sin no more." Even that Night He could turn and look on Peter. And that Closing Hour He still could find the second to say "Father, forgive them" and another for that Penitent, "Today shalt thou be with me in Paradise." And after His Victory He had not forgotten, for it was then He said, "Thomas" . . . and even since He has been calling us by name . . . we are His!

The Easter Gift in the Divine Commissioning is a perpetuation of this loving, *personal* ministry of comfort now bestowed on His little Company, and through all the after years on His servants.

How transcendent, but oh, how searching and humbling the thought: to minister the tenderness, the forgiveness, the healing, the Victory, *of Christ,* to some sin-sick, burdened soul. This committed to me;—in His Name, for His sake, to His glory, to bring to Him a soul, a life! "The ministry of reconciliation", the Victorious Christ, *God,* speaking through men, the pardon and the peace of the Cross and of the empty Tomb; to apply, to cure with, the Resurrection Balm. "Whose soever sins *ye* forgive, they *are forgiven* unto them," saith the Conqueror.

The Fifth : The Personal Touch

✛

MEDITATION : *Read*—St. Luke 15:3-7.

✛

SALUTATION

THEN saith He to Thomas, "Thomas . . ."

A strange man in that little Company; and yet, after all, was He?

As the hours build up that First Day, marks along its path are the "doubting ones", the "questioning ones", the "foolish and slow of heart"; only John, who looked in and went away, seemed at all *sure*. What of Peter?

But at eventide, "then were the disciples glad, when they *saw* the Lord." The Ten believed,—after they had seen,—but Thomas?

What a penalty he has paid ever since because he was not there when Jesus came! Men have called him "Doubting Thomas"! But at least he was straightforwardly honest! Does one wonder where he might have been, or why he was not there? Was he so disappointed, really so unbelieving, or so afraid? Even the glad testimony of the Ten, "WE have seen the Lord!" did not seem to help. Did he feel excluded?

"I will not believe . . . except . . ."!

[141]

What conditions one lays down for one's faith, service, allegiance; so important apparently when self-considered, but how infinitesimal when really in the Presence! But when Cross-weighed? Ah, "whosoever"!

Thomas carries his burden through the whole long week. Around him, all the while, gladness and faith; in his heart, gloomy clouds. How the little Company must have talked, calling so many things to remembrance; and how they rejoiced! But Thomas was on the outer edge of all this . . . "one of the Twelve" . . . a false note in the Easter chord. One of them a doubter, a demander?—still he clung to his doubt and he clung to his Companions! Think of what that intercourse meant . . . had he become stubborn Thomas? and was he hoping in his secret heart?

But he was there when Jesus came the second time. "Then saith he to Thomas." Even in these hours of triumph and glory Jesus has His personal, loving touch for just this one man.

Much the same way He had greeted Peter . . . "appeared unto Simon". . . . loving forgiveness! So He had met Mary at the sepulchre,—"Mary". . . "*My Master*". . . loving comfort! And now Thomas,— "Reach hither *thy* finger . . . *thy* hand . . ." "My Lord and my God". . . loving assurance!

This is the ever abiding ministry of Jesus to the heart. Only to be there when Jesus comes! . . . yes, with the troubled heart; for He will still it.

THE FIFTH: THE PERSONAL TOUCH

Is it peace for a longing, burdened soul? "Peace; it is I." Is it forgiveness? "Behold my hands and my side." Is it light and inspiration? "Receive ye . . ." Is it doubt of self? "Even so send I you." The Gift of the Personal Touch, His Ministry to me.

The Sixth : The Last Beatitude

✛

MEDITATION: *Read*—I PETER 1:3-9.

✛

SALUTATION

BLESSED are they that have not seen and yet have believed.

How much do I realize of what is in that "they"?—that it includes . . . you? . . . me?   Do I realize then, that we really were thought of that first Eastertide;—that very night when one human heart,—so much the pattern of multitudes since,—through the ministry of the Divine Love, was resolving its doubts into faith sure and strong, confessing and adoring?

A Divine couplet spans this brief period of days which is most intimately ours.   As Jesus enters the final hours, as He emerges victorious, He carried us with Him and He has brought us out!

In the night in which He was betrayed, the Divine Heart uplifted in intercessory prayer, was, in His everlasting love, covering all the days and years to come . . . and the day . . . and the hour, when *I* should come to Him!   "I pray . . . for them who shall believe on me through their word."   And now the benediction that is to rest on every one who cometh in

[144]

Him, "Blessed are *they* who have not seen and yet have believed." It may have been part of the answer to Thomas, but, none the less, it includes me.

How far the Highway has stretched since! How vast the Victor's Company that has traveled along! *Blessed!*—out of every nation and tongue and people! "Whom having not seen, ye love; in whom, though now ye see him not, yet believing, ye rejoice with joy unspeakable and full of glory."

The Seventh : My Gift to Him

✠

MEDITATION : *Read*—GALATIANS 2:30.

✠

SALUTATION

MY LORD and my God.
Thomas' instant response bursts forth like a
flash of pure light, revealing all; but, best of all, giving all. Here, no longer was he stopping to think;
no, not for a second about "evidence", or his demands,
or even about himself; that *he had had to do* while
his Lord was reaching out to him.

Can I, in some measure, comprehend this cry of his
which came from his soul? Can I realize his utter surrender? Can I truly value his outpouring of faith?

I am prone to forget how *human* these men were;
how these wondrous things affected them; how they
too had to come to Christ; how with them too, there
had to be a surrender of themselves.

Easter gifts, every one of them, but to Him; and a
great part of the glory of these gifts was in the way
in which they were given. The more it is given to
me to enter into these experiences, to comprehend their
fullness, their reality, the more my heart will go forth
feeling the urge all the while to give, *give,* GIVE!

THE SEVENTH: MY GIFT TO HIM

What? Can I, do I stop to ask?—either before His Cross,—or in the full glory of the Resurrection? What is my Easter gift to Him? Myself, my whole self, withholding nothing,—"humble love and loyal faith."

Lord, I will follow Thee, whithersoever Thou goest. Amen.

To-Morrow

✢

Jesus, still lead on,
Till my rest be won;
Heavenly Leader, still direct me,
Still support, console, protect me,
Till I safely stand
In the Fatherland.

✢